DESIGN
FOR HOW PEOPLE
LEARN

JULIE DIRKSEN

New Riders

DESIGN FOR HOW PEOPLE LEARN

Julie Dirksen

New Riders
1249 Eighth Street
Berkeley, CA 94710
510/524-2178
510/524-2221 (fax)

Find us on the Web at www.newriders.com
To report errors, please send a note to errata@peachpit.com
New Riders is an imprint of Peachpit, a division of Pearson Education

Acquisitions Editor: Wendy Sharp
Project Editor: Susan Rimerman
Developmental Editor: Wendy Katz
Production Editor: Becky Winter
Composition: WolfsonDesign
Indexer: James Minkin
Interior Design: Kathleen Cunningham
Cover Design: Mimi Heft
Illustration Production: Jessica Duff

ISBN-13: 978-0-321-76843-8
ISBN-10:   0-321-76843-4

9 8 7 6 5

Printed and bound in the United States of America

ABOUT THE AUTHOR

Julie Dirksen is an independent consultant and instructional designer with more than 15 years experience creating highly interactive e-learning experiences for clients from Fortune 500 companies and technology startups to grant-funded research initiatives. She has been an adjunct faculty member in the Visualization Department at the Minneapolis College of Art and Design, where she created and taught courses in project management, instructional design, and cognitive psychology. She gets ridiculously excited about things like learning applications of loss aversion or the way glucose is regulated in the brain and she's happiest whenever she gets to learn something new. You can find her online at www.usablelearning.com.

ACKNOWLEDGMENTS

There are many, many people I'm grateful to, including:

My distributed cognition network, without whom this book would be much worse, including Chris Atherton (book reviewer MVP & person who kept me from saying anything too stupid about brains, although if I did, it's not her fault), Dave Ferguson, Janet Laane Effron, Simon Bostock, Rebecca Davis, and Mags Hanley (who kept saying "That's great, Julie, but how do you *apply* it?").

The Peachpit/New Riders folks, Wendy Sharp, Susan Rimerman, Becky Winter and, most of all, the lovely and patient Wendy Katz.

The people who made it pretty—Jeremy Beckman, who was unbelievably generous with his time and creativity, Jess Duff, who made everything look better, and Leigh Simmons, who was really patient with me and who, even though I couldn't figure out a way to use it in the book, originated the phrase "Ninja cake time!" Also, the talented people who created the cover, interior design, and layout for the book.

Michael Allen, who is all you could wish for as a mentor, and Allen Interactions for their sabbatical program (which allowed me to write the original book outline), and for generously letting me use work I did at Allen Interactions (Bicycles!) in this book.

Kathy Sierra, who has been a huge inspiration and very supportive and is more responsible for this book than she probably knows.

All my incredible friends who have listened to me talk about this project for a LONG time, including my own Whuppass Girls—Mags (who rates a second mention), Samantha Bailey, and Lori Baker, along with Kathleen Sullivan, Lisa Boyd, Michele McKenzie, Ann Woods, and Lyle Turner. Also, Susan Quakkelaar and Lisa Stortz for their help and ideas, Jodi Hanson for her expert fashion advising, and the lovely and supportive Laura and Alexandra Nedved who are Max's other family.

All of the smart, interesting people in my professional network, including Tom Kuhlmann, who started me blogging and provided a role model for how to do it, Koreen Olbrish, who introduced me to the learning community on Twitter and who is an all-around rockstar, Will Thalheimer, who has been very generous with his considerable knowledge and advice, Cathy Moore, who I want to be when I grow up, and Jane Bozarth, who was very patient with my questions about all this book stuff. Also the rest of my #lrnchat PLN, the learning technology folks at Harrisburg University of Science and Technology, and the IST program at Indiana University.

All of my colleagues who have provided lots of advice, ideas, and interesting conversations, including Lester Shen, Carla Torgerson, Edmond Manning, Dan Thatcher, Karl Fast, Matt Taylor, the original Studio Z boys, and David Bael (& family).

The people who wrote the books on the inspiration bookshelf: Steve Krug, BJ Fogg, Scott McCloud, Jonathan Haidt, Robin Williams, Ralph Koster, Donald Norman, Stephen Anderson, Jesse Schell, and Kathy Sierra (who also rates a second mention).

The delightful women at the Blue Moon Coffee Shop, where this was largely written.

and

My parents and family, who managed to not freak out and even to be supportive when I said "I think I'm going to quit my job and freelance so I can work on a book."

FOREWORD

When working within the artificial intelligence group at Control Data Corporation on advanced learning systems, a colleague questioned why we were using such powerful systems as Cray mega computers for adaptive learning programs and learning simulations. He understood why meteorology and military reconnaissance applications needed them, but why educational systems? Meteorology dealt with vast amounts of data and yet needed to predict future weather quickly. Airborne reconnaissance had to compare visual data from separate flights and perspectives to recognize which objects had moved and which hadn't. But instruction?

Many people surmise yet today that instructional software can't make much computing demand. *How hard is it to present and score multiple-choice questions?*

I asked my colleague, what causes meteorology and reconnaissance to make heavy computational demands? He replied, *the extremely large amounts of data to be gathered and managed, the rapid analysis that was needed, and the need to visualize the results.* Hmm. It sounded familiar—like working with human learners. I asked him how much data he thought the human brain might typically contain and what level of complex analysis he thought it capable of. How would it compare to our largest computer? What level of common knowledge and reasoning had we achieved in our intelligent systems? How did that compare to working with people? What level of computation might be required to perform the tasks of a talented teacher and mentor?

With an estimated capacity of somewhere between 10 and 100 terabytes and with little-understood capabilities far beyond our most capable computers, the human brain is phenomenally complex. It's amazingly capable and surprisingly unpredictable. It's both rational and emotional. It's perceptive and yet selectively so. It can remember large amounts of data and yet has the advantages of forgetting. And each of us has a unique one.

The challenges of creating highly effective learning experiences are numerous. We're fortunate that humans are, in many ways, learning creatures. We are generally eager to learn. We intuitively know that knowledge is power. Skills turn knowledge into actionable advantages. We want skills and enjoy having them. But even with all these advantages, it isn't easy to transmit knowledge and build skills. Thinking of instructional technology as computer-delivered multiple-choice questions reveals how misunderstood the challenges are.

Regardless of how instruction is delivered—through instructor-led activities, e-learning, or other means—structuring effective learning experiences requires knowledge of *How People Learn.* So much instruction is developed and delivered through paradigms born of tradition rather than of knowledge. They are ineffective. They are boring. They are wasteful.

And yet, the science of the human brain is not a well-rounded guide for the preparation of learning experiences. Considerations, yes. Helpful, yes. Best practices, no. Eager for cookbook-like guidance, many look to research for widely applicable principles, yet most research findings are applicable only within narrow confines. When brain and learning research conflict with experience, experience is the better guide. Wisdom in learning design takes years to acquire. It takes focus, dedication, hard work, and an observant approach. Yet through this richness of varied context, experience has broad applicability that cannot be gained otherwise.

Through Julie Dirksen's extensive experience in designing learning experiences for wide varieties of learners in very different contexts, she clarifies why traditional instructional approaches are so ineffective. We learn from Julie's wisdom, for example, that while practice is important and so often omitted or minimized, there are more effective approaches to building long-term retention than simple repetition. We learn why words are a poor substitute for demonstration and example. We learn the power of context.

Traditional instructional design approaches focus heavily on content—getting it complete and accurate. Then making presentations as clear as possible. Then making assessments precise. Concerns about the learning experience, making it meaningful, memorable, and motivational, may not even enter into the discussion. I guess it's no wonder that we have so many boring and ineffective programs.

I'm delighted to have this witty, insightful, cleverly illustrated guide. My hope is that it will help designers shed the shackles of "tell and test" traditions from which learners are victimized by passive presentations of information followed by short-term retention tests. True, most of us had no choice but to learn from such instruction and survive. But there's no indication this should be the paradigm of choice. Watching Jay Leno's *Jay Walking* segments or *Are You Smarter Than a 5th Grader?* should be evidence enough that our educational traditions aren't working well. It's time to work smarter.

Michael W. Allen, Ph.D.
CEO, Allen Interactions Inc.
CEO, Allen Learning Technologies LLC

CONTENTS

INTRODUCTION

Think about the best learning experience you've ever had. What was it like?

Got one? I've asked this question dozens of times, and gotten a variety of answers. Sometimes the answer is that someone was really passionate about what they were learning, but the most frequent answer is:

Nobody ever says "I had the most amazing textbook" or "There was this *really great* PowerPoint deck!"

That suggests that a lot of what makes for a great learning experience is not about the content, but is about the way the content is taught. In fact, a class can cover the same material but be very different, depending on how the material is taught:

So what's the special sauce? How are the two experiences different? When it's two different teachers, some of the differences are due to personality or charisma, but those aren't usually the only differences. And when it's an e-learning course, there's no teacher at all. How is a really good e-learning course different from just reading a textbook online?

Even more important, what's the difference between a learning experience that's effective versus one that gets forgotten as soon as the learner is done? Even "awesome" classes are useless if the learner doesn't do something different afterwards. While some learning experiences are "learning for the sake of learning," I won't really address those in this book. (Disclaimer: I work with adult learners, usually in a professional setting, so while the book will address examples from multiple contexts, the majority will relate to adult learning experiences.)

For me, the goal of good learning design is for learners to emerge from the learning experience with new or improved capabilities that they can take back to the real world, that help them do the things they need or want to do. If your learners are on a journey from novice to expert, how can you help them along that path?

Expert!

Novice

This book looks at some of the things involved in designing great learning experiences:

Chapter 1: Where Do We Start?
If learning is a journey, what's the route like for your learners, and what's the gap between where they are and where they need to be? Sometimes that gap is knowledge, but just as often the gap can be skills, motivation, or environment. Learn how to identify each of these.

Chapter 2: Who Are Your Learners?
Your learners see the world differently than you do, and to design effective learning experiences, you need to understand their view of the world.

Chapter 3: What's The Goal?
The best learning experiences are designed with a clear destination in mind, but sometimes a clear destination can be harder to pin down than it seems. Learn how to determine your destination with accuracy.

Chapter 4: How Do We Remember?

Learn about how the brain works to focus on and retain information.

Chapter 5: How Do You Get Their Attention?

The first prerequisite for learning is to get your learners' attention. Learn strategies for getting past the distractions and helping your learners to focus.

Chapter 6: Design for Knowledge

The most common type of learning experience focuses on teaching knowledge. Learn strategies to make this as effective as possible.

Chapter 7: Design for Skills

If you ask the question "Is it reasonable to think that some can be proficient without practice?" and the answer is "No," then you aren't teaching information, you are teaching a skill, and skills require practice. Learn strategies for helping your learners get the practice they need to develop skills.

Chapter 8: Design for Motivation

If you've ever heard a learner say the words "I know, but..." then you are probably not dealing with a knowledge gap, but rather a motivational one. Learn strategies for getting your learners not only to learn more, but also to do more.

Chapter 9: Design for Environment

We can get people to hold more information in their heads, or alternately, we can learn better ways to make information available to them in their environment, so they can get it when they need it.

Chapter 10: Conclusion

WHERE DO WE START?

(In which we learn that it's not always about what people *know*, and that you shouldn't use a suspension bridge to fix a pothole)

THE LEARNER'S JOURNEY

Are the following statements true or false?

- If you teach someone about how smoking is bad for them, they'll stop smoking.
- If someone goes to a management training class, they'll be good managers.
- If someone takes a really good web design class, they'll be a good web designer.
- If you teach someone the right way to do something, they won't do it the wrong way.

Did you think any of those statements were completely true?

No, of course you didn't, because there are a lot of complicating factors that influence whether a person succeeds or not.

Learning experiences are like journeys. The journey starts where the learner is now, and ends when the learner is successful (however that is defined). The end of the journey isn't just knowing more, it's *doing* more.

So, if that journey isn't just about knowing more, then what else is involved? What else needs to be different in order for someone to succeed?

WHERE'S THE GAP?

There's a gap between your learner's current situation and where they need to be in order to be successful. Part of that is probably a gap in knowledge, but as we began to discuss above, there are other types of gaps as well.

If you can identify those gaps, you can design better learning experiences.

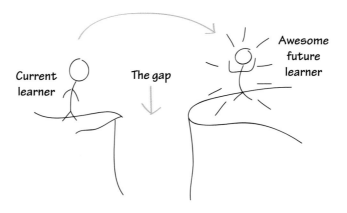

For example, consider the following situations. What could be the gaps for each of these scenarios?

- Alison is a project manager for a web design company, and she's just agreed to teach an undergraduate project-management class at a design school. Her students will mostly be students in the second year of the creative design program. Most of the students are 18–19 years old and are taking the class because it's a requirement for their degree.
- Marcus is teaching a two-day workshop on database design for a new database technology. This is the second time he's taught the workshop, and he's revising it because it was too basic the first time around.
- Kim is designing a series of e-learning courses for a large global company that recently merged with a smaller company. The two companies are buying a new purchasing system to replace each of the companies' older systems. The employees of the smaller company will also need to learn the procedures from the larger company.

For each of these, think about how should the learner be different—what could and should they do differently—before and after the learning experience?

In the case of Alison's class, it could be that the gap is just a matter of knowledge: A student comes in not knowing anything about project management, and comes out knowing a lot more about project management.

But is a lot of project management knowledge all that's needed to make somebody a capable project manager? There's more to good project management than just knowing information. And of course that will hold true for much more than Alison's class. Let's take a look at some of the kinds of gaps can exist for learners.

KNOWLEDGE GAPS

Before we examine other types of gaps, let's take a closer look at knowledge or information gaps.

In most learning situations, it's assumed that the gap is information—if the learner just had the information, then they could perform.

I recently worked with a client on a project to teach salespeople how to create a product proposal for potential clients. The salespeople need to be able to choose which product best meets a client's needs, and then to select a series of options so the product is optimally customized for that client.

We were working on revising an old course, in which there were about four slides that listed each of the product features.

And that was it.

Hmm.

If you were learning this, do you think this equation adds up?

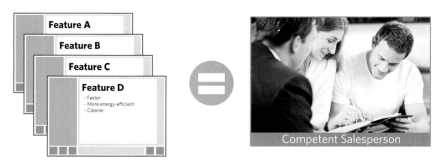

No, of course not—even if the learners memorized the exact information on each of those slides, that wouldn't mean they were able to use it well. But certainly, having the right information is part of the equation.

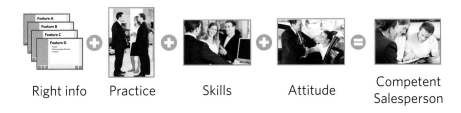

Right info Practice Skills Attitude Competent Salesperson

Information is the equipment your learners need to have in order to perform. Having information doesn't accomplish anything by itself. Something is accomplished when the learner *uses* that information to do things.

Basically, you want your learners to have the right supplies for their journey:

But you also want your learners to know what to *do* with that information. Having the information without knowing how and when to use it is like having a really great tent you don't know how to put up or spending a lot of money on a really terrific camera but still taking cruddy pictures because you don't have the abilities needed to use it.

If the *only* thing your learner is missing is the information, then your job is actually pretty easy, especially living in this information age. There are lots of easy, cheap ways to convey information.

Another benefit of the information age is that you don't necessarily need your learners to carry all the information the whole way on their journey. If they can pick up less critical information as they go along, you can focus initially on the more critical knowledge that they really need to have with them the whole way.

As for all the rest of that information, think about how you can cache it for your learners, so they can easily pick it up when they need it. If they get the information when they really need it, they'll also appreciate it more.

We'll take a closer look at different ways to supply information to your learners in later chapters.

SKILL GAPS

Let's say I've figured out the start- and end-point of my journey, I've got it all mapped out, and I have all the gear I need: Am I now ready to hit the 2,000-mile Appalachian Trail?

Probably not.

Anything more ambitious than a gentle afternoon hike is probably beyond me at the moment. So what would I need to be ready to tackle the Appalachian Trail? Would more gear help? More route planning?

Not really. The only thing that is going to get me ready for a major, multi-day hike is a lot of hiking, and even a less ambitious goal would require practice and conditioning.

Time spent on practice devices like elliptical machines or stairclimbers would probably help towards the goal of a major hike, but in the end, tackling an expert-level hike would require a lot of practice on less challenging hikes. For example, even if I sat down and memorized an Appalachian Trail guidebook, it still wouldn't be a good idea to try it if I didn't also have the necessary conditioning and skills.

Learners in all disciplines are frequently in the same situation. They get handed the knowledge in a book or a class, but don't get the opportunity to practice and develop skills.

The
Appalachian
Trail

Skill vs Knowledge

Having a skill is different than having knowledge. To determine if something is a skill gap rather than a knowledge gap, you need to ask just one question:

Is it reasonable to think that someone can be proficient without practice?

If the answer is Yes, then it's not a skill, but if the answer is No, then you know you are dealing with a skill, and your learners will need practice to develop proficiency.

Here's a little game you can play to help you in your planning: Let's play Skill/Not a Skill:

Action	Skill?	
Saving a file in MS Word	Yes	No
Playing Skeeball	Yes	No
Giving performance reviews	Yes	No
Filling out a timesheet	Yes	No
Calming an irate customer	Yes	No
Building a database	Yes	No
Designing a brochure	Yes	No
Making mac & cheese from the box	Yes	No
Problem-solving a missing supply order	Yes	No
Programming the shopping cart widget for a website	Yes	No

I don't really think saving a MS Word file, filling out a timesheet, or making macaroni and cheese would really be considered skills (although you might be able to convince me on the last one), but I believe everything else on the list would require practice to do well.

Just like you would never expect someone to tackle the Appalachian Trail on their first hiking trip, you can't expect learners to pick up new skills without practice, and that practice needs to be part of the learning journey you design.

MOTIVATION GAPS

If somebody knows what to do, but chooses not to do it, that's a motivation gap.

There are a number of reasons for motivation gaps. It could be that the person doesn't really buy into the outcome or destination.

It could be that destination really doesn't make sense.

It could be due to anxiety, or concern about change.

Sometime people get distracted, or unfocused.

Sometimes people just aren't interested in making the effort.

And sometimes people fail because they lack enough of the big picture to guide their own success.

I was recently talking with a colleague about learner motivation, and she argued that it wasn't the learning designer's problem. She felt that people brought their own motivation to the table, and that it really wasn't in the designer's control. I agreed with her to the extent that you can't force a learner to be motivated, but that there are ways to help support motivation in a learning design.

Design decisions influence people's behavior. For example, in a recent study (Song, 2009), people were given lists of tasks. The only difference between the two lists was the font used. Participants were asked to rate how easy or difficult they thought the task would be to perform.

Tasks shown in easier-to-read fonts were rated by the participants as being easier to perform. The group given the lists in a hard-to-read font rated those tasks as being harder to perform.

Lie on your back with knees bent and feet resting on a flat surface.
Cross arms over your chest or clasp them behind your head.
Tuck your chin against your chest.
Tighten your abdominal muscles and curl up.

Lie on your back with knees bent and feet resting on a flat surface.
Cross arms over your chest or clasp them behind your head.
Tuck your chin against your chest.
Tighten your abdominal muscles and curl up.

This is a fairly subtle way of influencing a learner's motivation (and some research suggests that things read in a harder-to-read font may be easier to remember, ironically), but there are countless design decisions you might make while designing a learning experience that will influence your learner's motivation. For example, do you dwell on all the things that can go wrong? That might be a good way to prepare the learner for troubleshooting, but might also convince them it's not worth the effort in the first place.

CHANGE: THE SPECIAL MOTIVATION GAP

One of the things you may need to consider in your learner's journey is if the new learning is going to require *unlearning*.

When Tiger Woods changes his golf swing, his game takes a hit for a while until it (usually) improves again. This is a fairly difficult process, because it not only involves adding the new technique, it involves unlearning the old technique.

As we gain proficiency in something, the memories around that proficiency become streamlined in our brains. We get more efficient in how we access and use the information and perform the procedures around that task. This is an important part of learning—if it didn't happen, then riding a bike for the thousandth time could be just as difficult and exhausting as riding a bike for the first time.

This streamlining process is a natural blessing for learning, but it poses a difficulty for *re*-learning, because when your learning requires the learners to change or replace an existing practice, then you have to deal with the fact that your learners already have *momentum.*

They are already going in a particular direction, at a pretty good clip. And they have many parts of that automated. When you automate something, you can relegate control of that task to a part of brain that doesn't require much conscious attention.

There are a lot of brain resources going to that task when it's new. When you are first learning to ride a bike, for example, you need to put a good amount of your conscious attention to the task of staying upright.

When you become proficient, you don't have to consciously think things like "I'm tipping! Omigosh, whaddoldo? whaddoldo?" Instead, your body just adjusts left or right without your having to think about it, and you can concentrate on other important thoughts like "Oh crap, that log wasn't there the last time I came down this route!"

But this has significant implications for learning.

Let's go back to our example with Kim from the beginning of the chapter.

Kim is designing a series of e-learning courses for a large global company that recently merged with a smaller company. The two companies are buying a new purchasing system to replace each of the companies' older systems. The employees of the smaller company will also need to learn the procedures from the larger company.

Who do you think is going to have a bigger challenge learning the new system? The group used to the existing procedures, or the group learning the new procedures?

Both groups are probably going to struggle with the new computer system, because it won't be what they are used to, but obviously the second group is also going to have the extra challenge of learning a new procedure as well.

Old information and procedures get in the way of new information and procedures. Have you ever noticed when someone is not a native speaker of your language, and the word order in their sentences can be a little weird? It's likely that this is an example of what is called L1 interference, which is when somebody's knowledge of their first language interferes with their ability to speak second language.

If people are going to change the way they do things, then they are going to stumble over those old habits. If they automatically do certain things, they are going to have to make a conscious effort to *not* do those things. This is more difficult to than just making a conscious effort to do something new, and, not unimportantly, it can make people grumpy.

If you are asking your learners to change an existing habit or practice, you are probably going to have some motivation issues to contend with. In those instances, there are a couple of things to be aware of.

First, change is a *process*, not an event. You absolutely cannot expect someone to change based on a single explanation of the new practice. They need time and repetition to ease back on the old habit, and start cultivating the new one.

Second, backsliding and grumpiness are part of that process—they don't mean the change has failed (although that can happen too), but they are frequently an unavoidable part of even successful changes.

ENVIRONMENT GAPS

So, let's say your learner has good directions, is fully prepared, is in good shape, and is raring to go. Nothing should stop them now, right?

Sometimes the path itself isn't set up to let people succeed:

Environment gaps can take a lot of different forms in an organization. For example, if you want somebody to change their behavior, does the process support it?

Are there materials, references, and job aids to support the learner when they get back to their work environment?

Do they have everything they need in terms of materials, resources, and technology?

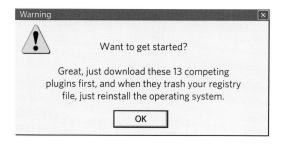

Are people being incented and rewarded for making the change?

Is the change being reinforced over time?

COMMUNICATION GAPS

Sometimes someone is failing to perform isn't due to a lack of knowledge but because they have bad directions.

This isn't really a learning issue—this is a miscommunication issue. It can happen for all sorts of reasons. Sometimes the person communicating the direction doesn't really know where they want people to go.

Or sometimes, the person communicating knows where they want people to go, but can't adequately communicate that knowledge.

Occasionally, the person giving the directions says one thing, but either doesn't support it or really intends something else.

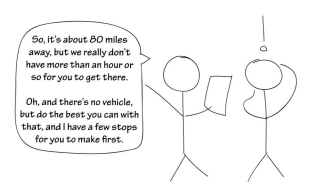

So, for example, let's say that one of Alison's students is using all his shiny new project-management abilities on a project building a website for his uncle, but a few weeks into the project, it's not going very well.

The website is behind schedule, the person doing the graphics can't finish them, and the design for the whole gallery section is a mess.

Does that mean that Alison's student didn't really learn everything he needed to know about project management? Maybe he's making rookie mistakes, despite everything he learned in class?

Or could it be that the uncle is the client from hell who didn't say that he was leaving the country for a month, changes his mind frequently, and forgot to mention that he wanted a gallery section on the website in any of the initial meetings? That might be why.

So how much of this a learning issue? None of it, really, but communication issues can sometimes masquerade as learning issues.

We need training to improve the level of customer service.

We're getting killed on the customer satisfaction surveys.

But the surveys say that what they are really unhappy about is that they spend 10 minutes on hold, and wind up in loops in the automated phone system.

Um, customer service training won't actually fix any of that...

Frequently, the best you can do in those situations is document the issue, handle the politics, and do no harm to the learners, if possible.

IDENTIFYING AND BRIDGING GAPS

So, when you are mapping out the route, you need to ask yourself what the journey looks like.

Knowledge
- What information does the learner need to be successful?
- When along the route will they need it?
- What formats would best support that?

Skills
- What will the learners need to practice to develop the needed proficiencies?
- Where are their opportunities to practice?

Motivation
- What is the learner's attitude towards the change?
- Are they going to be resistant to changing course?

Environment
- What in the environment is preventing the learner from being successful?
- What is needed to support them in being successful?

Communication
- Are the goals being clearly communicated?

Questions To Ask

There are a variety of strategies to help identify the gaps. Here are a few for starters:

- Ask "What do they actually need to *do* with this?" (If you get the answer "They just need to be aware of it," then ask "Yeah, but, what do they actually need to *do* with this?" *again*.)
- Follow a novice around and see what they do; then follow an expert around and see what they do differently.
- Ask yourself if the person *would be able to* do something if they wanted to badly enough. If they answer is yes, it's not a knowledge or skills gap.
- Ask the question "Is there anything—anything at all—that we could do, besides training, that would make it more likely that people would do the right thing?"
- Ask "Is this going to involve changing the way they do things now?"
- Ask "What is the consequence if somebody does it wrong?"
- Ask "If someone is getting this exactly right, what would that look like?"
- Ask "Is it reasonable to assume that someone will get this right the first time out, or will they need to practice to get proficient?"

EXAMPLES

Let's identify the gaps in a few scenarios.

SCENARIO 1: MARIANNA

Marianna is a newly minted supervisor for her company's IT support department. She was a great IT support person and now she's been promoted, supervising five other IT support workers.

Her HR department sends her to a new-manager training class, where she learns all about the paperwork necessary for managing hourly workers, and about a coaching model for providing good and timely feedback to her direct reports.

Marianna's first few weeks are a bit rocky. She is swamped by the paperwork demands, and has to work really hard to keep up. Other supervisors seem to stay on top of their paperwork, so Marianna isn't really sure what she's doing wrong. A couple of her employees are starting to come in late, and she's reluctant to confront them directly about it, because she doesn't want it to seem like she got all bossy just because she was promoted. She tries to use the coaching method she was taught, but while it works a little with one of the problem employees, it doesn't work at all with the other, and as Marianna gets busy, she doesn't really finish all the steps to the coaching process. She's not that convinced it was helpful, anyway.

Marianna's manager is aware that she's struggling somewhat, and is thinking of arranging more managerial training for her.

Which of the following gaps are relevant for Marianna?

- Knowledge
- Skills
- Motivation and Attitude
- Environment
- Communication

> **"Diagnosis" for Marianna →** This is almost certainly not a knowledge problem. Marianna appears to know *what* to do, but needs a lot more guided practice to develop the skills that will help her perform the task efficiently and well. She has as some attitude and motivation gaps that make her reluctant to use what she knows. Specific coaching from her manager will probably be more helpful than additional classes, and it's possible there are elements in her environment that could be changed to help her keep up with the paperwork.

SCENARIO 2: MARCUS

Let's revisit Marcus from the beginning of the chapter, and take a closer look at his situation.

Marcus is teaching a two-day workshop on database design for a new database technology. This is the second time he's taught the workshop, and he's revising it because it was too basic the first time around. It was kind of a rough first teaching experience for Marcus.

Originally, he spent a lot of time on the principles of database design, and got out his old textbooks to cover basic design principles, like how to normalize a database.

When he taught the class, though, it turned out that most of the people in the class were actually experienced database designers who were there specifically to learn the new technology. Some of the students complained about the functionality of the technology, and Marcus felt caught out when students wanted him to explain *why* things had to be done a particular way.

Which gaps does Marcus need to think about for his audience?

- Knowledge
- Skills
- Motivation and Attitude
- Environment
- Communication

> **"Diagnosis" for Marcus →** His first time around, Marcus focused more on database design skills, which his audience didn't really need. His audience does have a knowledge gap around the functionality of the new system, and there are some attitude/motivation gaps that are likely the product of his learners being forced to do things differently than they are accustomed to. If Marcus can focus on getting his audience comfortable with the specific software functionality and how it can be useful for them, his second class will probably go better.

SCENARIO 3: ALISON

Let's also revisit Alison from the beginning of the chapter.

Alison, a project manager for a web design company, has just agreed to teach an undergraduate project-management class at a design school. Her students will mostly be students in the second year of the creative design program. Most of the students are 18 or 19 years old and are taking the class because it's a requirement for their degree.

Which gaps does Alison need to think about for her audience?

- Knowledge
- Skills
- Motivation and Attitude
- Environment
- Communication

"Diagnosis" for Allison ➜ There's no indication of a communication issue, but Alison will need to accommodate pretty much all of the
other types of gaps. Her students don't have a lot of work experience
to draw on, and probably don't have much or any project-management
knowledge. They will need to develop skills to be able to apply what she
teaches, and will need to have elements in their environment to support
what they learn. Given that it's a required course, and that her students
are primarily art and design students, she needs to think about how to
encourage their attitude and motivation.

WHY THIS IS IMPORTANT

Several years ago, I was working on a proposal for a prospective client. The client
had come to the company I worked for and said, "We have a problem with a
high employee turnover rate. We want a training course on the history of the
company to reduce that rate."

We gently suggested that if they had a high turnover rate, it was probably not
primarily due to employee ignorance of company history, and would they like
us to look into other possible causes?

Yeah, we didn't get that contract. Oh darn.

In Chapter 3, we'll take a look at how to set good goals for learning, but before
you get to goals, it's really important to define the gap you are trying to fill or
the problem you are trying to solve.

If you don't start with the gaps, you can't know that your solution will bridge
them. You can build a suspension bridge to cross a crack in the road, or try to
use a 20-foot rope bridge to span the Grand Canyon.

One of my all-time favorite clients was a group that did drug and alcohol prevention curriculums for middle-school kids. When they were initially explaining
the curriculum to me, they talked about how a lot of earlier drug-prevention
curriculums focused on information ("THIS is a crack pipe. Crack is BAD.").

Now, does anyone think the main reason kids get involved with drugs is a lack of
knowledge about drug paraphernalia, or because no one had ever bothered to
mention that drugs are a bad idea?

Instead, this group focused practicing the heck out of handling awkward social
situations involving drugs and alcohol. Kids did role-plays and skits, and brain-
stormed what to say in difficult situations. By ensuring that the curriculum

addressed the real gaps (e.g., skills in handling challenging social situations), they were able to be much more effective.

If you have a really clear sense of where the gaps are, what they are like, and how big they are, you will design much better learning solutions.

SUMMARY

- A successful learning experience doesn't just involve a learner knowing more—it's about them being able to *do* more with that knowledge.

- Sometimes a learner's main gap is knowledge, but more frequently knowledge and information are just the supplies the learner needs to develop skills.

- Use the question "Is it reasonable to think that someone can be proficient without practice?" to identify skills gaps. If the answer is no, ensure that learners have opportunities to practice and develop those skills.

- You need to consider the motivations and attitudes of your learners. If they know how to do something, are there other reasons why they aren't succeeding?

- Change can be hard because learners may have deeply ingrained patterns they have to unlearn, and you need to expect that as part of the change process.

- The environment needs to support the learner. People are much less likely to be successful if they encounter roadblocks when they try to apply what they've learned.

- Sometimes it's not a learning problem, but rather a problem of communication, direction, or leadership. Recognizing those instances can save a lot of effort in wrong directions.

- If you have a well-defined problem, you can design much better learning solutions. It's always worth clearly defining the problem before trying to define the solution.

REFERENCES

Ellickson, Phyllis and Daniel McCaffrey, Bonnie Ghosh-Dastidar, and Doug Longshore. 2003. New inroads in preventing adolescent drug use: Results from a large-scale trial of project ALERT in middle schools. *American Journal of Public Health*. 93(11):1830-6.

Song, Hyunjin and Norbert Schwartz. 2009. If It's Difficult to Pronounce, It Must Be Risky. *Psychological Science* 20 (2): DOI: 10.1111/j.1467-9280.2009.02267.x

WHO ARE YOUR LEARNERS?

(In which we learn that our learners are not necessarily like us, and also the importance of tidy closets)

Understanding your learners is part of designing good learning experiences. If you don't understand your learners, unfortunate things can happen.

> Check out this awesome tutorial I did on the new customer service procedures. It's all interactive video conversations. Very cool stuff.

> That's for the call center in Bogata? Dude, none of those computers have sound cards.

> Okay, everybody ready for this 90-minute class on how to use voicemail?

Voicemail Basics

> Er...we can just read these laminated cards and figure it out for ourselves. We just came because you need to give us our login IDs...

> Because you already know the basics of loan-processing heuristics, I'll just jump right into the system changes...

> Um....I'm a new hire...

> What's a heuristic?

So, what do you want to know about your users? First of all, you might want some basic demographic information (such as age, gender, job, or role). You can usually get that information via a survey, or sometimes organizations already have that kind of data on file.

You may also want to know things like their reading level or how they use technology, if those things are relevant to the subject you are working on. You can also use surveys to find those things out, or you can talk to some representative learners (which is always a good idea).

In addition to those types of audience demographics, you also want to get the answers to a few key questions:

- What do your learners *want*?
- What is their current skill level?
- How are your learners different from you?

We'll look at these questions in this chapter. Additionally, we'll take a look at learning styles, and also what methods you should use to gather the information you need to design learning for your audience.

WHAT DO YOUR LEARNERS WANT?

Highly motivated learners will learn, regardless of the quality of the learning experience. Similarly, unmotivated learners are a challenge even for the best teachers. But the more you can consider your learners' attitudes and motivations, the better you can tailor the learning experience.

You want to consider the question of what your learners want from a few different angles. Think about why they are there, what they want to get out of the experience, what they *don't* want, and what they like (which may be different from what they want).

WHY ARE THEY THERE?

In considering the "why are they there?" questions, let's take a look at some of the types of learners you might encounter:

Would be happy with a list of what to do and a quick run through

On a schedule

Really not interested in your story about that one time with the pineapple...

"Tap tap"

The "Just tell me what I need to know" learner

Hey! Check this out!

Brings lots of motivation to the table

Rampant curiosity

Is actually interested in your story about that one time with the pineapple...

The "Hey! This is cool!" learner

Highly motivated—really highly motivated

Not interested in the backstory

plumbing for dummies

A trial-and-error learner

The "I need to solve a problem" learner

May need to be convinced that the material is useful

Someone for whom the material may not actually be useful

Motivated by other factors like grades or completion

The "This is a required course" learner

Wired for distractions

Short, distributed attention

Thinks they multi-task, but really just switch focus a lot

MAC

The "Oooh – Shiny!" learner

That's not the way we've always done it...

That sounds hard...

Needs to be convinced that the change will be doable and useful

Needs time to acclimate and safe opportunities to practice

The "I fear change" learner

Uh huh, uh huh, uh uh, uh huh... oh wait, that's new! uh huh...

Really, really doesn't want to sit through the beginner material (really)

Understands quickly and gets a lot of the subtleties

Doesn't need the whole backstory

The "I pretty much know all of this already" learner

Which type are you? All of the above, most likely—depending on the subject matter and context. You've probably been all of these types at one time or another. You might have been a "required course" learner in math and a "hey, cool!" learner in music (or vice versa).

Ultimately, we are all the "What can I get from this?" learner. We want to know why a learning experience is useful or interesting to us. Regardless of type, people want to have purpose and be able to *do* something with what they are learning.

INTRINSIC VS EXTRINSIC MOTIVATION

Let's take a look at two people who are learning to program in Java. Pat is an **intrinsically** motivated learner, while Chris is **extrinsically** motivated.

Intrinsically motivated learners are interested in the topic for its own sake, or have a specific problem they are trying to solve. Pat wants to use Java to *do* something specific.

Extrinsically motivated learners are motivated by an outside reward or punishment. Any kind of learning that is "required" is likely to be extrinsically motivated. Chris's reasons for learning Java are very different.

As you might imagine, intrinsic motivation kicks extrinsic motivation's ass.

The same way any one person can be a different kind of learner depending on the subject matter and context, a learner's motivation can also be intrinsic or extrinsic depending on the circumstances. For example, someone's motivation during the annual sexual harassment prevention seminar may be pretty extrinsic (it's required), but may be become a lot more intrinsic later (when an employee comes to them with a sexual harassment complaint).

HOW DO YOU DEAL WITH EACH TYPE?

Depending on what type of learners you have, there are strategies that you can use to improve the learning experience.

Design strategies for teaching intrinsically motivated learners include:

- **Saying "Thank you" to the learning gods.** Seriously, your life is going to be much easier.
- **Making sure your learners have time to work on their own problems.** You may have some standard activities or challenges that everyone needs to do, but you will get a lot better mileage if learners are working on problems that are meaningful to them.

- **Leveraging your learners as teachers.** Intrinsically motivated learners are going to learn a lot on their own, and will learn even more if they share that knowledge. As they do so, it will expose other students to a wider variety of possible applications. It also takes the pressure off of you to be the only source of information and energy. Score!

Design strategies for teaching extrinsically motivated learners include:

- **Scouring their situation for intrinsic motivators.** Is there anything— *anything*—that they find intrinsically motivating about the subject matter? Ask lots of questions about what they might do with the information. Try to tie it back to relevant, real-world tasks.
- **Looking for pain points.** If your learners are unfamiliar with the material, they won't be able to make connections between their aggravations and the solutions you are offering, but if you can figure out what annoys them and show them how they can alleviate that annoyance, you can transform extrinsic into intrinsic in moments.
- **Avoiding extensive theory and background.** You may find that academic stuff fascinating, but extrinsically motivated learners would rather stab themselves in the eye with the free pen. Stick with specific examples and challenges that directly relate to real-life scenarios. In fact, this is usually true for *all* learners. If you've got a lot of backstory, and you can't say exactly why it's important, then you should cut it. Seriously—highlight and delete (or at least move to the appendix or resource section).
- **Using interesting hypothetical problems to awaken their intrinsic motivation.** If you start with a genuinely interesting challenge or puzzle that the learner needs to solve, their extrinsic motivation will start to drift towards more a more intrinsic motivation, like puzzle-solving or winning. Just keep in mind that when I say "interesting" I mean "interesting to them."

Here's an example of a design challenge for extrinsically motivated learners. Several years ago, I was looking at an e-learning course designed for high-school students to take online. The courses had lovely, flashy graphics and animation. I opened the first course, which was on statistics, and the first thing that happens was a very enthusiastic announcer saying "Welcome to this course. Let's start with the....History...Of...Statistics!!"

How many high school students do you think are going to be intrinsically motivated by the History Of Statistics?

Yeah, not so much. In fact, it's safe to say that without the extrinsic rewards and punishments, they wouldn't be anywhere near this topic.

> **So here's your redesign challenge** → If you want to get a little intrinsic motivation from this bunch, how could you introduce the topic differently?
>
> Some possible ideas include:
>
> - Use famous or controversial statistics (e.g., "50% of all marriages end in divorce") and have students research what those numbers really mean, and how they are derived.
> - Look at statistics that impact their lives (census data, school funding, etc.).
> - Make it about money (that's always interesting).
> - Have them decide which used car to buy based on statistical data.

YOUR LEARNERS WANT TO NOT FEEL STUPID

A few times over the years I've had this basic conversation with clients:

> **CLIENT:** We want to do a basic overview for people. Essentially, we want to do "Our Topic for Dummies." But we can't say "Dummies" of course. We can't suggest that people are dumb.
>
> **ME:** I don't think people take it that way.
>
> **CLIENT:** Regardless, we'll have to call it something else.

It's an interesting question, right? Why would anyone buy a book for "dummies"? Clearly, people do buy them, and it's probably not because they think they aren't smart.

I've always argued that the whole point of the dummy/complete idiots/beginner's books is that instead of calling you dumb, their main selling point is that they promise to NOT make you feel stupid.

If I pick up a guide to wine that already assumes I know the different between a cabernet and a merlot, then I'm already feeling a little sheepish about my own ignorance. But if I pick up a book that doesn't assume that I know the difference between riesling and tap water, then when I do know something, I can feel superior without risk.

A friend of mine is a game designer who is now designing e-learning programs, and when he talks about game design, he says "My job as a game designer is to make the player feel smart." I think the same is true for learning designers. Your job is to make your learners feel smart and, even more important, they should feel capable.

The "I don't want to feel stupid" learner

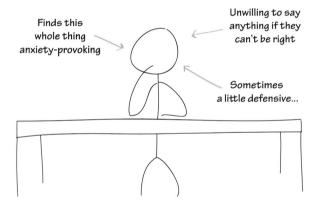

It's fine to challenge your learners—this isn't about making it easy for them. Things that are too easy aren't a good way to learn either. But you don't want to have your learners feel shame about what they do and don't know. Instead, you want to give your learners a safe path into the material.

Dan Meyer, a math teacher and blogger (http://blog.mrmeyer.com), describes the process he uses when introducing a problem to students:

We take guesses—What do you think? What do you know is a wrong answer? I'll ask a struggling learner for a wrong answer. Give me a number that's too high. Give me a number that's too low. I'm involving students at a very low investment that has a huge return.

Some ways to engage wary learners:

- **Leverage what they already know.** Can you take advantage of any knowledge they already have about the topic?
- **Give them some early success.** What can be something they can achieve early on? Is there some accomplishment that they can tackle with the material within the first lesson?
- **Create safe places to fail.** Can they practice or self-assess in a private or non-judgmental environment?

If you do this well, then when they do start to succeed, your learners will feel like they *own* the subject matter. If you pull that off, then *you* win as the learning designer.

WHAT DO YOUR LEARNERS LIKE?

In addition to knowing what your learners want, you also want to ask what they like. My game-designer friend also advocates finding out about your learners' preferences:

> *...You can see that if we are going to focus on developing software that our users want and like, it's essential that we know and understand our audience, not just the subject matter.*
>
> *I would suggest that you research the brands, hobbies, and media (television, films, games, websites, etc.) that your target audience enjoys. This should give you a better idea of the aesthetics and interactions that your learners like and want. (Raymer 2011)*

If you think about it, this makes perfect sense. If your audience loves basketball or knitting or opera or reality television, why wouldn't you want to utilize that to make your learning design more engaging for your learners? Obviously, your entire audience won't like exactly the same TV shows, but if you can find a common thread, you can use that in your design.

WHAT IS THEIR CURRENT SKILL LEVEL?

One of the things you need to consider when you are finding out about your learners is their current skill level. Basically, you want to know how steep the climb is going to be for them.

Are you asking your learners to do this?

Or this?

And how much of an effort are you asking your learners to make?

This question is complicated by the fact that while you have some control over the difficulty of the material, much of the outcome is determined not by your design, but by the learners' ability.

For example, you may be building something that seems—to you—to function at a fairly reasonable level of effort.

But to a complete novice, it feels pretty steep.

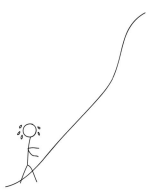

If someone is already an expert, then the material may require no effort at all.

Let's say you're working with a novice jogger, a pretty good amateur runner, and an experienced professional marathoner. Each person would need not only a different *level* of instruction, but actually would need very different approaches.

For a novice jogger, the learning experience you need to provide would include:

- Lots of guidance
- A careful introduction that doesn't go too quickly in the beginning
- A structured experience that has immediate, achievable goals
- Increasing self-confidence
- A gradual progression of difficulty with opportunities to rest
- Coaching and feedback on how they are doing

For a proficient recreational runner, you would include:

- Some practice of new concepts
- Advanced topic information
- Coaching and shaping for improvement of existing behaviors
- Much more autonomy

The expert marathoner would want:

- Somebody to hold out the bananas and water and then get the hell out of the way
- Really expert coaching
- Information about specific challenges (e.g., the characteristics of a particular route)
- Some help with measuring progress (mile marking / timekeeping, etc.)
- Full autonomy
- The opportunity to act as a resource by teaching or coaching others

Aside from the bananas, these characteristics hold true for almost any discipline. A more beginner audience needs a lot of structure and guidance, and a more advanced audience needs more autonomy and resources that they can choose to access as needed.

SOME LEARNERS ALREADY KNOW A LOT

We've already looked at the idea that the same content can look pretty steep to a novice but be more like this for an expert:

People are faster on the straightaways.

If somebody is already an expert, they can pretty much zoom along, until they come to a gap in their knowledge or hit an unusual or novel concept or dilemma. Then they need to slow down, absorb the needed information or skill, and then they can be off and running again.

Unfortunately, a single learning design is frequently expected to accommodate many different levels of learners.

This means that all the things you built into the learner's journey to support novices (careful guidance, lots of practice, slowly helping them build their mental model before adding in content) are pretty much guaranteed to make the expert absolutely *nuts*.

This is the equivalent of being the experienced flyer standing in the TSA security line with your laptop out, liquids in a bag, shoes off, and carry-on ready to go, trapped behind what appears to be a Grandma who hasn't flown since 1972 and an entire daycare of small children with all their associated paraphernalia.

Whole spectrums of learners frequently get shoved through the same learning experience for reasons of budget or convenience.

If that has to be the case, consider the following suggestions:

- **Don't make them hate you.** Don't make every part of the learning experience required for everybody. Just don't. Really. This means don't make people sit through classroom training they don't need—make parts of the classroom experience optional or take-home. This also means that you shouldn't lock down a menu in an e-learning environment, forcing people to go through it in order or require them to wait until the entire audio narration has played before you let them advance to the next screen.
- **Consider pull vs. push**. Novice learners frequently don't know what they don't know, but experts frequently have a pretty good idea. You can generally trust experts to get the information they need if you make sure that it's easily available and applicable.

> **Pull** means you provide the resources, lessons, and reference materials and the learners choose when they need them. You want to make them as easy to find and as accessible as possible, but you don't need to force them through it.

- **Leverage their expertise.** These are smart people! Figure out ways to make use of that. Can they coach novices? Can they have special access to the course to add their own experiences and stories to make the course more vivid for novices? If you can figure out a way for them to use their expertise to enhance the journey for others (and learn a few things along the way), then they will have a whole different level of engagement with the material.
- **Embed some of the novice information.** If, for example, you're providing vocabulary for the more novice learners in an e-learning program, make that vocabulary available by rolling over the word rather than spelling it out in the main content. That way, it's there if your novice needs it, but it doesn't slow down the more knowledgeable learners.
- **Let them test out (maybe).** One of the most common tactics for addressing varying difficulty levels is to say "We'll have a pre-test! So if people really know the information, they don't have to take the course!" Here's the thing with this. This is a perfectly reasonable approach IF you think you can create a genuinely effective pre-test that measures knowledge or skill. Honestly, I've not seen that many good pre-tests. Either they tend to be trivia questions, or they tend to be so easy that any reasonably astute person could guess their

way through to a passing score. It's *hard* to write a good assessment. And if you are trying to assess a *skill*—something that had to be developed over time and through practice—well, how likely are you to be able to do that with something like a multiple-choice quiz?

Skills can be assessed, but they usually need to be assessed through observation of competencies rather than multiple-choice tests (unless the competency you are assessing is the ability to take tests).

- **Ask "Do you need anything?" and then get out of their way.** If you are supporting an expert marathoner, you don't say "Hey, let's wait for some of the newer folks to catch up" or "Have you seen this brochure on ways to motivate your training regimen?" Instead, you say "Need anything? Banana? Water? No? OK—see you at the next mile marker then!" The same goes for learning resources: Figure out what they need, make sure they have access, and then stop bothering them.

SCAFFOLD THE INCLINE

What if the topic is too complicated for novice learners to really tackle without hopelessly oversimplifying the content? What if putting the content into a realistic context means that context is overwhelming to the user?

One of the ways to deal with this is *scaffolding*. Basically, you can build supports to make the incline less steep. Then you can gradually reduce those supports until learners can handle the incline on their own.

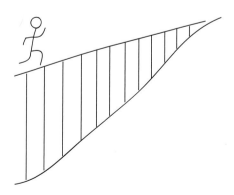

Good scaffolding acts like training wheels; it allows learners to accomplish the difficult task in a safely supported way. Ideally, it doesn't reduce learners to bystanders, but gives them the support they need to complete tasks they wouldn't otherwise be able to do.

Examples of ways to scaffold:

- **Reduce the complexity of the environment.** Let's say you want to teach someone about the controls in a plane cockpit, but it's too overwhelming for a novice learner. To scaffold their learning experience, you could fade out all but a few of the key controls for the first few scenarios, and then gradually add controls back in as the learner becomes more proficient and competent.
- **Use walkthroughs.** Have the learner go through the whole process with a simplified case. For example, if you want to teach students about the scientific research process, have them work through a very simple research problem with step-by-step guidance and pretty obvious results, and then move on to more complex cases.

  Another example: I once created a fairly complicated environment for salespeople to learn a specific sales process by selling technical products to several virtual customers. Their very first scenario was a short and slightly silly example where they sold snowsuits in Hawaii, which gave them the opportunity to learn the interface and the sales process without worrying about the technical content right away.
- **Provide supports.** If possible, embed easily accessed references in the experience. For example, have samples, definitions, or help documentation right at hand so the learners can have the support they need while in the midst of trying to accomplish the task.

HOW ARE YOUR LEARNERS DIFFERENT FROM YOU?

The first thing you need to know is:

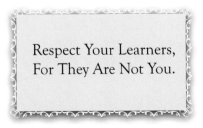

Respect Your Learners,
For They Are Not You.

Seriously, I'm getting this made up as a bumper sticker. It's one of the most important things you can remember.

Let me give you an example. Several years ago I was reading an article about different work styles, and the article categorized people into four broad types, with questions to help you identify your own type.

I was reading the description of my type and nodding a fair bit. My type enjoys problem-solving? Absolutely. Yep, I like new challenges. Yes, the opportunity to learn new things *was* a good motivational reward for me.

And then I stopped.

And I looked at the other three types, while one of those cartoon light bulbs was going off over my head. I love learning new things (it's how I wound up in instructional design), *but not everybody feels the same way.*

Probably not that much of a revelation, but I was genuinely struck by it. You mean there are people who are mostly comfortable with the safe and familiar? People for whom learning something new is scary or uncomfortable? Or people who primarily regard it as a nuisance, or a necessary evil to be dispensed with or circumvented as quickly possible? Really?

Whoa.

I was seriously ashamed of myself—I had been subconsciously assuming that my experience was the norm. Quite possibly you never shared that particular blind spot, but everyone inevitably thinks about teaching through the filter of their own experience. What learning experiences were effective for you? How do you like to learn? Surely other people would also like to learn in similar ways, right?

Mostly, that's right, actually, but it's important to keep in mind that not everybody will have the same focus and motivation. Also, your learner does not see the world the same way you do.

WHAT IS YOUR LEARNER'S CONTEXT?

Consider your learner's context for the material.

You have a lot of context for the material you know, and your learners frequently have quite a bit less context.

Read the following example:

> First, you will need to provide support above the usual level. If you do not have a device for this elevation, you will need to obtain one. Before you provide the elevation support, you will want to decrease the later resistance for all the critical contact points. After the elevation device has been utilized, you can complete the rotation of the critical contact points, and exchange the impacted element. You will then want to re-engage the critical contact points and remove the device. You may continue to use the replacement element. If it is not adequate for long-term use, you may want to repair or replace the original element, at which point you will need to repeat the process.

Was this difficult to follow? Did you have to force yourself to concentrate to understand or process what was being said?

OK, now try this version. Take a look at this picture and then read the paragraph again.

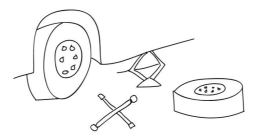

First, you will need to provide support above the usual level. If you do not have a device for this elevation, you will need to obtain one. Before you provide the elevation support, you will want to decrease the later resistance for all the critical contact points. After the elevation device has been utilized, you can complete the rotation of the critical contact points, and exchange the impacted element. You will then want to re-engage the critical contact points and remove the device. You may continue to use the replacement element. If it is not adequate for long-term use, you may want to repair or replace the original element, at which point you will need to repeat the process.

Did it make more sense the second time around?

The tire-changing example was based on an experiment (Bransford 1972). They also used a similar example where the task was doing laundry, and they had three groups:

- A group that was told it was laundry before they read the paragraph
- A group what was not told the example referred to laundry
- A group that was told that it was laundry only after they'd read the paragraph

Unsurprisingly, the group that understood and remembered the most was the group that knew what the example was about before they read the paragraph. They were able to understand and retain the information specifically because they already had a mental picture about laundry that they were able to use to parse the information.

This is important to keep in mind because whenever you have a lot of knowledge about something, you have a picture in your mind, and your learners may not.

HOW MUCH YOU KNOW VS HOW MUCH THEY KNOW

Let's say you are teaching an introductory course on something you know a lot about. But of course you can't talk to a novice audience the same way you'd talk to a colleague. So what's the bigger barrier? Is it how much they know (not much)? Or is it how much *you* know (a lot)?

Well, sometimes the barrier genuinely is how little your learner knows:

But just as often the barrier is how much you know and—more importantly— how hard it is for you to remember what it was like *not* to know it. Have you ever had somebody explain something technical or complicated and just not been able to follow what they are telling you? If so, you know that you don't want your learners to experience that.

It can sometimes be hard to avoid, because of the way we mentally organize information.

WHY YOUR BRAIN IS LIKE A CLOSET

Think about a subject in which you have expertise. What kind of mental model do you have? This kind?

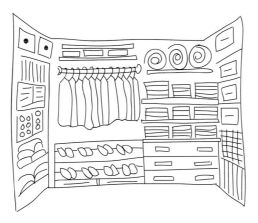

Or this kind?

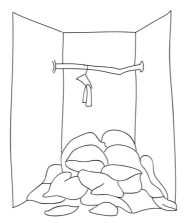

If you are the expert, it's likely that you have the first kind of mental model—pretty orderly, with a lot of different categories, distinctions, and a sophisticated way of organizing the information. If you are the novice, you have a lot less structure around the information you know.

If somebody hands an expert a blue sweater to put in the closet, that expert will be able to decide pretty quickly where to put that sweater because they already have a structure in place (on the sweater shelf, next to other winter clothing, ordered by weight or style or even color).

But when you hand content to a novice learner, that person is likely to look perplexedly at the piece of information that they have no context for, shrug, and toss it onto the pile of other information accumulating on the floor of their closet. We've all had those training experiences where you get a flood of information, and all you can do is try to keep up.

The bigger problem comes when you want someone to *retrieve* the information. As the expert, you have all sorts of ways to pull out a particular piece of information—you can check sweaters, check winter clothing, check casual wear, or check things that are blue. At the same time, your learner is pawing randomly through their pile, with no other strategy than to try really hard to remember.

HOW DO YOU HELP NOVICES STRUCTURE THEIR CLOSETS?

The first thing you need to do is help your learners build a few shelves.

There's no way that any single class or training program is going to get them all the way to your mental model, and you shouldn't try (that's just as bad as burying them under a flood of multi-colored laundry). But you can definitely provide some context for the information that you are going to give them.

Here are a few ways to help your learners build shelves:

Use a high-level organizer. Start them with some structure that will help them organize what follows. This could be a road map of the broad categories, an overview of the basic principles, or an acronym or a mnemonic device. This gives them some shelves on which to start putting information on.

Use visuals. Visual information contains several extra cues that give your learner more hooks for storing and retrieving the information.

Use a story. People have amazingly sticky memories for well-told stories, particularly ones that arouse emotions.

Work through problems. One way experts categorize information is by how they can use it to solve a problem, or how they can apply it. Working through problems helps novices start developing their own similar structure.

Have learners design shelves. Give learners the information as a specific task, and have them decide how it should be organized. Ask them how they would present it if they had to teach it to others. You can then have them compare their organization to the expert view and let them think about what they would do differently in future.

Use a metaphor or an analogy. Compare the relevant subject matter to something that your learners are already familiar with, so you can leverage the storage and retrieval capability of one of their existing mental models. It's frequently a good idea to use something common and everyday that the learner can't help but be familiar with, like, oh, say—a closet.

It's worth mentioning that while it's more common to have experts teaching novice learners, that's not always the case. Sometimes experts teach other experts, or, most difficult, an expert is teaching an audience of widely mixed levels of expertise.

As we've already mentioned, people who already have a lot of expertise really don't need a lot of setup—they know where the blue sweater goes, and just want to get on with it.

Learning experiences for people who already have a lot of expertise should be efficient, and should be more "pull" than "push." Let them decide when they need it and how much.

Whenever possible, you want to make sure that a knowledgeable person has a fast-forward lane, so they can get the necessary information without having to wade through all the material they already know.

THE EXPERIENCE FILTER

All learners, both novice and expert, filter their new learning through their past experience. Humans are sense-making animals. We will try to interpret and make explanations for things we don't understand.

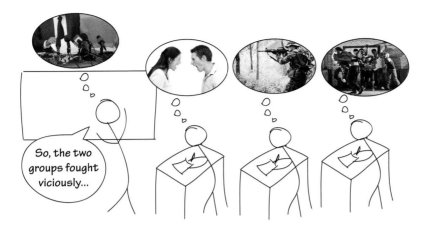

This is OK, and a perfectly normal part of learning. Everyone's understanding is colored by their previous experience, and therefore everybody's understanding of the same material will be a bit different.

Sometimes, though, that can lead to critical misconceptions, as here:

BARISTA-IN-TRAINING: This customer wants one of the St. Patrick's Day Peppermint Wasabi Double Espressos, and he's paying with a credit card. I haven't done a credit card yet.

EXPERIENCED BARISTA: (thinks "OK, he's the first one today to order that disgusting seasonal specialty") OK, mark it as a specialty order, and I'll show you how to run the credit card.

Hours later...

EXPERIENCED BARISTA: (checking receipts) What the hell? 107 specialty orders? Is that right?

BARISTA-IN-TRAINING: I think so—a lot of people paid with credit cards today.

HOW CAN YOU KNOW WHAT YOUR LEARNERS ARE THINKING?

Unless you can mind-read, you need to make sure the information flows both ways.

The traditional lecture classroom is probably the most common, familiar model that people recognize for how learning works: The teacher pours information to the heads of learners.

The problem with this is that the information is only flowing in one direction.

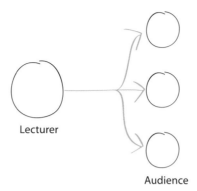

Lecturer

Audience

A lecturer could talk for days, and not have any idea what misconceptions his or her students might have. Eventually, in traditional classrooms, misconceptions may turn up on an assignment, but only long after the information has settled into the learner's mind, and the ideal opportunity to correct the misconception has passed.

A better model is an interactive one that has information flowing in both directions:

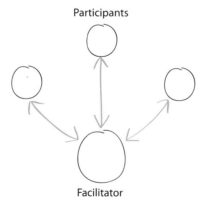

Participants

Facilitator

Regardless of the learning venue (classroom, e-learning, informational website), it's best to have as interactive an experience as possible. Ideally, you would construct opportunities to see how your learners are interpreting and applying what they learn, so you can correct misconceptions, extend their understanding, and identify ways to reinforce the learning.

LEARNING STYLES

But wait, what about the "I'm an auditory, visual, tactile, kinesthetic, conceptual, social" learner? Don't we also want to know our audience's learning styles?

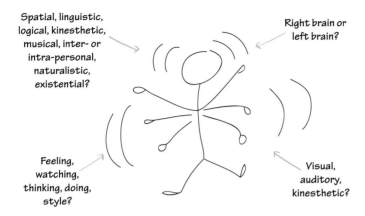

Spatial, linguistic, logical, kinesthetic, musical, inter- or intra-personal, naturalistic, existential?

Right brain or left brain?

Feeling, watching, thinking, doing, style?

Visual, auditory, kinesthetic?

Maybe you are familiar with the concept of learning styles. For example, you've probably heard of someone being described as a "visual learner."

Basically, the idea espoused by learning-style advocates was that if we could identify individual differences in how people learn, we could provide them with learning experiences that best match their learning styles and improve learning outcomes.

There are many intelligence- or learning-style inventories. Here are a few of the more prominent ones:

- Gardner's Multiple Intelligences—Howard Gardner proposes that people have different kinds of intelligences (spatial, linguistic, logical, kinesthetic, musical, interpersonal, intrapersonal, naturalistic, and existential), rather than a single type of IQ (intelligence quotient).
- VAK or VARK—This model proposes that people have inclinations towards learning styles like visual, auditory, reading, or kinesthetic learning.
- Kolb's Learning Styles Inventory—David A. Kolb proposes a set of learning styles (converger, diverger, assimilator, and accommodator) based on preferences for abstract vs concrete and active vs reflective learning.

WHAT CAN I DO WITH LEARNING STYLES?

Not much. Sorry, but the scientific evidence of effective use of learning styles is pretty weak (at the time of writing this book). There are a couple of assumptions that can't really be proved—first, that somebody's learning style can easily be measured, and second, that there is a practical way to adapt the learning experience to those styles. Technology may solve this problem eventually, but for now we don't really have effective examples of this.

I bring this up because learning styles are pretty popular, but haven't proven to be very effective. That may change in future, as people investigate better ways to assess and apply learning styles.

Still, all is not lost; there are some useful ideas you *can* get from the learning styles conversation:

- **Not everyone learns the same way.** Even if you can't adapt a learning situation to someone's unique learning style, you can create learning experiences that incorporate a variety of approaches. This also helps keep a learning experience interesting, and provides a variety of memory triggers. Varying the learning styles also battles against people's tendency towards habituation (more on this later).
- **There are different kinds of intelligence.** I used to teach art students, and they loved learning about multiple intelligences because it validated their skills and abilities that fell outside of the traditional definition of IQ.
- **We are more alike than we are different.** Excepting certain physical impairments, we all learn from visual, auditory, and kinesthetic methods, and we have all the different types of intelligence at varying levels.
- **You may want to vary the learning approach depending on the subject being learned.** While there is little evidence to support customizing learning to a particular learner's style, there is some evidence that suggests that you should adapt the learning approach to the content being taught. At a minimum, use common sense to match the approach to the task. You wouldn't want your car mechanic trained via audiobook, right?

METHODS FOR LEARNING ABOUT YOUR LEARNERS

So how do you find out about your learners? There are several good books on the topic of analysis for instructional design (start with Allison Rossett's *First Things Fast*), and there's a lot to be learned from the field of user experience about how to research your audience.

I'm not going to get into a lot of detail about this, but there are a few key practices that I believe are crucial for good audience analysis:

- Talk to your learners
- Follow your learners around
- Try stuff out with your learners

TALK TO YOUR LEARNERS

This may sound unbelievably obvious, but in my experience, a lot of learning gets designed without talking to learners. As an instructional designer, I've had a number of projects where I talk to project stakeholders, to trainers, to managers, and to subject matter experts. Unless I insist on it, I rarely get to talk to the actual learners. To be fair, most of these experts have a lot of experience with the subject matter and with the learners, so they are great sources of information, but they also have pretty sophisticated closets. You should talk to all of those people AND you should talk to your learners.

Here are a few reasons why:

- **They will tell you how it works, not how it should work.** Stakeholders, managers, and experts are often very vested in the "right" way to do something. They'll tell you how the manual says to do it, but your learners will frequently tell you what happens in the real world. In theory, loan-closing requests are scheduled "by the book," but actually the customer service people use a particular shortcut. In theory, programmers write their own subroutine for a particular function, but really everyone goes to the same open-source code site and copies the free code that's posted there. You may still need to teach the official version, but you can create better scenarios and support materials if you know how it really happens.
- **They can tell you where it hurts.** Your best friend when designing learning is someone who is currently learning the topic or has just recently learned it. They are very clear on what was confusing or difficult to wrap their heads around. They can tell you what made sense to them when they were trying to

understand the new concepts or ideas. They can tell you what was easy and what they are still struggling with.

- **They can give you examples and context.** Learners' comments, complaints, suggestions, and ideas can give you all the little details necessary to create really good learning scenarios. Your experts can sometimes do this as well, but sometimes their examples get a little out of date (it may have been a while since they did it themselves), while your current learners frequently know what the current challenges are.

Some questions you should ask learners:

- Why are you learning this?
- How will learning this help you (how are they motivated)?
- What are the biggest hassles or challenges you experience (in relation to the topic)?
- What are some examples of when you've had problems?
- What was the hardest thing for you to learn?
- What were the easy parts?
- What could make it easier for you?
- How do you use this information now?
- What do you wish you knew when you first started?
- Can you walk me through it?
- What does a typical example look like?
- What crazy exceptions have you seen?

FOLLOW YOUR LEARNERS AROUND

Sometimes this important process is called job shadowing, and in the user experience community it's often referred to as contextual inquiry, but it basically amounts to follow your learners around in their actual environment.

This is not focus groups, email surveys, or phone interviews. This is face-to-face in the environment where they will be using the learning. Could be an office, a factory, their computer setup in their den—wherever. If you can do only one type of audience analysis, do this (you can always ask your questions along the way).

Why is following your learners around important?

- **Context, context, context.** You want your learning to create contextual triggers that will allow learners to remember things later. We'll talk more about this in Chapter 4, but people remember more in a similar environment than they do in a dissimilar environment, and the more context (visual or situational) that you can leverage, the better people will remember.

- **Even new learners have started to build some shelves.** Even if you are talking to new learners, they've already started to develop their closets, which means that they've probably already automated some of the steps in their brains. If you're asking them about what they do, they are already starting to gloss over details, but if you watch them in their actual environments, you see what's happening, and can stop and get more information, e.g., "Can you tell me more about that step you just did?"

- **Juicy details.** If you are trying to create good examples or scenarios for learning, you can get the best details from seeing people in their actual environments. If you know about their world, you can create better examples, scenarios, and activities much more easily.

TRY STUFF OUT WITH YOUR LEARNERS

Frequently, analysis gets done, and then the learning designer goes away and designs the learning, and it gets distributed to the learners. If someone is teaching, face to face, they get a decent amount of feedback in the process of teaching the class. If the learning is delivered by other people, or if it is e-learning, sometimes very little feedback reaches the learning designer.

Try stuff out with your learners along the way. If you have an idea for an activity, see if you can get a few people to try it out. Create prototypes, do user testing, have pilot tests.

This is not the same thing as showing it to someone and getting their feedback. Getting people to review your materials can be useful, but everyone fills in the gaps with their own understanding. Nothing will show up gaps like trying stuff out. Have a quick and dirty test of a lesson or an activity. Watch users try an e-learning program. Do a pilot of a class with a small sympathetic audience.

Are there parts where people get confused? Do certain parts drag? Do you find yourself talking for a long time in the middle? Was your test audience confused by the instructions for an activity? Testing your learning design early and often will allow you to fix these things before you get in front of your official learners. All the learning theory in the world won't help you as much as testing your learning designs and fixing the problems.

There are a few reasons why this is important:

You think you are being clear, but you *know* how it's supposed to work. Anyone who designs anything gets a certain amount of tunnel vision. If you try things out, you can find out what does and doesn't make sense to a learner before you've invested too much time and effort into what might be a wrong direction.

You'll get good ideas. You'll think of all sorts of good ways to refine the design that you could never have come up with in a vacuum.

It's more efficient in the end. If you regularly try things out, you can do lean versions, and just fill in where there are issues. This means you can create much shorter, more efficient lessons than if you try to guess what your audience does and does not know.

SUMMARY

- You want to know about your learners—not just about their demographics, but about their motivation, likes and dislikes, skill level, and about how they understand the world.

- Provide more structure for your new learners, and more resources and autonomy for your experienced learners.

- Don't just hand your learners information, but instead help them construct and organize their framework for that information.

- Learning experiences should be two-way interactions, so you know when learners understand correctly, and when they don't.

- All of the theory in the world won't help you as much as spending time in your learners' world, and testing your designs early and often.

REFERENCES

Bransford, J.D. and M. K. Johnson. 1972. Contextual prerequisites for understanding: Some investigations of comprehension and recall. *Journal of Verbal Learning and Verbal Behavior* 11:717-726.

Chi, M. T. H., P. Feltovich, and R. Glaser. 1981. Categorization and representation of physics problems by experts and novices. *Cognitive Science* 5:121-152.

Coffield, F., D. Moseley, E. Hall, and K. Ecclestone. 2004. *Learning styles and pedagogy in post-16 learning. A systematic and critical review.* London: Learning and Skills Research Centre.

Fleming, N.D. and C. Mills. 1992. Not Another Inventory, Rather a Catalyst for Reflection. *To Improve the Academy* 11:137.

Gardner, Howard. 1999. *Intelligence Reframed: Multiple Intelligences for the 21st Century*. New York: Basic Books.

Kolb., David A. and R. Fry. 1975. Toward an applied theory of experiential learning. *Theories of Group Process*, C. Cooper (ed.). London: John Wiley.

Meyer, Dan. YouTube video on real-world math, http://www.youtube.com/watch?v=jRMVjHjYB6w.

Paschler, H., M. McDaniel, D. Rohrer, and R. Bjork. 2010. Learning styles: Concepts and evidence. *Psychological Science in the Public Interest* 9:105-119.

Raymer, R. 2011. Gamification: Using Game Mechanics to Enhance eLearning. *eLearn magazine* (http://elearnmag.acm.org), in review.

3
WHAT'S THE GOAL?

(In which we learn that buildings learn like people do, and that you should let your learners drive the car, not just ride along)

DETERMINE GOALS

Whenever you are designing a learning experience, it's critical to have clear goals defined. If you don't know where you are and where your learners need to be, you can't figure out how to get them there.

If you don't have a clear destination, you can't plot a clear path, and you certainly can't communicate that path to your learner:

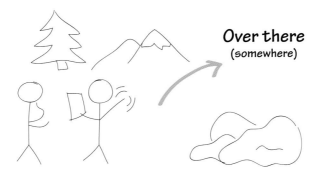

Over there
(somewhere)

In determining the path for your learner, you want to do these things:

- Identify what problem you are trying to solve
- Set a destination
- Determine the gaps between the starting point and the destination
- Decide how far you are going to be able to go

IDENTIFY THE PROBLEM

In the first chapter we talked about identifying the gaps. You want to start with the gaps when identifying the destination.

UH HUH, AND *WHY* DO THEY NEED KNOW THAT?

I've had some variant of this conversation with clients many times over the years:

CLIENT:	The salespeople just need to understand the basics of insurance underwriting/cellular service/cloud computing. That's the learning objective.
LEARNING DESIGNER:	OK, sure, and why is it important they know that?
CLIENT:	Well, they just need to be grounded in the basics.
LEARNING DESIGNER:	Uh huh. And what will they actually do that with information?
CLIENT:	They just need to know it.
LEARNING DESIGNER:	And what bad thing could happen if they don't know it?
CLIENT:	Well, they'd look stupid in front of clients.
LEARNING DESIGNER:	Ah! Great. So maybe the learning objective is something more like "Salespeople should be able to answer customer questions accurately."
CLIENT:	Yeah, I guess that makes sense.

Before you start designing a learning experience, you need to know what problem you are trying to solve.

A lot of learning projects start with the goal, rather than the problem, but that puts you in the position of solving problems you don't actually have, while failing to address the real issues.

For example, let's look at this goal, and some possible solutions:

Goal	Possible Solutions
Marianna will be able to give appropriate and timely feedback to her staff.	Marianna could watch another supervisor model good feedback.
	Marianna could take an e-learning course on coaching and providing feedback for employees.
	Marianna could role-play feedback scenarios with other staff members.

All of those solutions could potentially address the stated goal. Let's take a look at the same set of choices with the gap identified first.

Gap	Goal	Possible Solutions
Marianna was recently promoted, and is struggling with giving feedback to people who used to be her peers (skills/ motivation gap).	Marianna will be able to give appropriate and timely feedback to her staff.	Marianna could watch another supervisor model good feedback. Marianna could take an e-learning course on coaching and providing feedback for employees. Marianna could role-play feedback scenarios with other staff members.

The goal is still valid, but now some of the possible solutions are better than others—observing other supervisors and role-playing become better solutions than taking a knowledge-based course.

Here's another example:

Goal	Possible Solutions
Members of the repair staff need to be knowledgeable about basic principles of electricity.	Course on introduction to electrical physics Simulation for troubleshooting common electrical problems Lesson on dangers of electricity Simulation lesson on making electrical circuits

Let's take a look at this same one with the gaps:

Gap	Goal	Possible Solutions
Newly hired repair staff members frequently lack the knowledge and skills to troubleshoot customer electrical problems safely.	Repair staff needs to be knowledgeable about basic principles of electricity.	Course on introduction to electrical physics Simulation for troubleshooting common electrical problems Lesson on dangers of electricity Simulation lesson on making electrical circuits

Some questions to ask to help identify the problem:

- "What bad thing will happen if they don't know this?"
- "What are they actually going to do with this information?"
- "How will you know if they are doing it right?"
- "What does it look like if they get it wrong?"
- "So why is it important they know that? Uh huh, and why is *that* important?" (repeat as needed)

BREAK IT DOWN

Sometimes a topic is just too big to be precise:

Students need to learn to be better managers.

That's like saying "Meet me in Africa." It's a destination, but it doesn't help you book a flight. In those instances, you want to start breaking it down:

Students need to schedule restaurant employees so all shifts are adequately covered.

Students need to provide appropriate feedback to an employee who is chronically late for work.

Once you start breaking these down, you can formulate much more specific routes and destinations to get where you need to go.

SOMETIMES THERE IS NO PROBLEM

Sometimes there really is no problem to be solved.

I might take a class in film appreciation just for my own satisfaction, but I wouldn't expect the learning objectives to make me a professional film critic. A community-education course on Taiwanese cooking, a painting class at a local art museum, or even a high-school French class aren't really set up in response to a "problem."

Not all journeys are about the destination. Some are about taking a nice walk somewhere pleasant, or about getting in shape. Even when the learning isn't in response to a problem, it's likely to be in response to a need or desire.

What do the learners want or need to get out of the experience? If you are creating learning experiences that are primarily for enrichment, you will still create better experiences if you consider and define those wants or needs.

SET THE DESTINATION

After you've defined the problem, you need to define your goal(s).

The more specific you can be about this, the better you can design the path to get there. For example, let's say someone is teaching a Java programming class and the objective is:

Students will understand how to program in Java.

This is a learning objective pretty much guaranteed to make a formally-trained instructional designer's head explode:

There are actually a number of problems with this learning objective, but let's start with the use of the word "understand."

It's a totally reasonable place to start—of course we want our learners to understand, but there's no visible way to see if someone "understands." It's hard to design for something as fuzzy as "understand," so we need to define it more.

One way some people get around this is by using "doing" words in their learning objectives:

Students will be able to explain the value of computation for modeling and simulation.

Students will be able to describe the proper use of method calls.

Students will be able to define and describe the use of core data structures such as arrays, linked lists, trees, and stacks.

They use words like define, describe, and explain because those are observable actions—you can witness someone describing, defining, or explaining.

Of course, this is hedge; it doesn't really get you around the problem, unless you are having people memorize and recite definitions. In fact, it's almost as difficult to determine if they can *define* something as it is to know if they *understand* something. Besides, you don't actually care if they can *define* it—you want to know if they can *do* it.

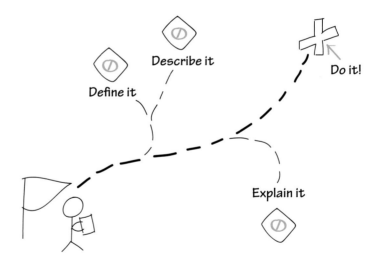

Using those kinds of approximations is basically saying "I don't know exactly how to explain what I want, but I'm pretty sure this gets them in the neighborhood."

Ultimately, since we don't really care what they know, we care what they can *do*, the learning objectives should reflect that:

> *The student will be able to create a simple, fully functional user interface that collects customer data and transmits that data to the database.*

So, when you are creating learning objectives, ask yourself:

- Is this something the learner would actually do in the real world?
- Can I tell when they've done it?

If the answer to either of those questions is *no*, then you might want to reconsider your learning objective.

Learning Objective	Would do?	Can Tell?
Learner should be able to identify all the criteria necessary to select the correct product for that client.	Yes/No	Yes/No
Learner should be able to list all common Dutch prepositions from memory.	Yes/No	Yes/No
Learner should understand project-management roles and responsibilities.	Yes/No	Yes/No
Learner should be able to create a website that works on the five most common web browsers.	Yes/No	Yes/No
Learner should be able to state the legal definition of sexual harassment.	Yes/No	Yes/No
Learner should be able to identify if a complaint meets the definition of sexual harassment, and be able to state the reasons why.	Yes/No	Yes/No
Learner will understand the limitations of JavaScript as a programming tool.	Yes/No	Yes/No

OK—now let's take a look at each of these. While you look at the answers, think about how you could change the learning objective to make it meet both criteria.

Learning Objective	Would do	Can Tell
Learner should be able to identify all the criteria necessary to select the correct product for that client.	Yes, this is probably a real-world task.	Yes, there are a number of relatively simple ways to assess if the learner can do this.
Learner should be able to list all common Dutch prepositions from memory.	No	Yes, this would be easy to assess.
Learner should understand project-management roles and responsibilities.	Maybe. The goal is so broad and fuzzy, it's hard to say yes or no definitively.	This would be extremely difficult to assess. It would probably be best to break this learning objective down into smaller objectives.
Learner should be able to create a website that works on the five most common web browsers.	Yes	Yes
Learner should be able to state the legal definition of sexual harassment.	No	Yes, although some clarification would be necessary to say for sure. For example, do you need a word-for-word definition, or just the major criteria?
Learner should be able to identify if a complaint meets the definition of sexual harassment, and be able to state the reasons why.	Yes; this is a task that someone might need to do in the real world.	Yes
Learner will understand the limitations of JavaScript as a programming tool.	Not really. It's a little fuzzy and broad, and could be made much clearer.	No

So if we wanted to fix that last objective, how we could make it better?

Original objective:

> *Learner will understand the limitations of JavaScript as a programming tool.*

Some possible revisions:

> *Learner will be able to identify the best programming tools for a specific task and be able to state the reasons why.*

or perhaps:

> *Learner will be able to state whether or not JavaScript is an appropriate pro-gramming tool for a specific task and give a correct rationale for the decision.*

There may be times when it's not feasible to have real-world tasks. For example, if you are teaching someone nuclear physics, there may be some conceptual material that just doesn't have an analogous real-world task, but is necessary to understand in order to tackle later concepts. Still, even in those instances, there's probably something the learner is supposed to *do* with the information, even if it's just to use it to understand something else.

These recommendations are guidelines, not unimpeachable rules. Use your judgment. If you feel like you need to do backflips to get a learning objective to work, then that's usually a clue that you need to unpack it more—either break it down, or keep asking *why* until you've uncovered the real purpose.

HOW SOPHISTICATED SHOULD YOUR LEARNER BE?

When setting your goals, consider how much you want your learner to actually learn. There are a couple of ways to think about this.

The first way is to think about how sophisticated or complex do you want your learners' understanding to be. One scale for this Bloom's Taxonomy (this is the later version, revised by Anderson & Krathwohl in 2001):

- Remember
- Understand
- Apply
- Analyze
- Evaluate
- Create

So, for example, if someone is reading *The Non-Designer's Design Book*, an excellent book on the basics of graphic design, they would learn about the graphic design principles of Contrast, Repetition, Alignment, and Proximity (which adds up to a nicely memorable acronym).

If we looked at this from the perspective of the taxonomy, it might be like this:

Taxonomy	A Way The Learner Might Do This
Remember	Tell somebody what the acronym is and what each item stands for.
Understand	Explain what each principle means.
Apply	Organize the elements of a web page using the four principles.
Analyze	Look at a print advertisement and explain how each of the four principles is being used in the design.
Evaluate	Expertly critique several different advertisements based on their use of the four principles.
Create	Create a print or web layout from scratch.

The items are intended to becoming more cognitively demanding as you go (e.g., "remember" should be easier than "evaluate"), and some learning designers view the list as a progression (e.g., you have to understand before you can analyze).

Logically, the idea that this is a progression makes sense, but it's not a recipe for a learning design. For example, analyzing a series of advertisements could be a good way to understand the principles, or guiding learners through the creation of a print advertisement could be a good way to learn an application.

In fact, you could create a great lesson by inverting the order completely:

Taxonomy	A Way The Learner Might Do This
Create	Give the learners some elements (product photo, copy, logo) and have them create a mockup of an advertisement.
Evaluate	Have learners compare their advertisements to a few professional examples, and have them discuss what they did right and wrong.
Analyze	As students are pointing out design elements that work, group those elements on a whiteboard into the four design principles.
Apply	Have the students go back and fix elements in their original advertisement based on the design principles.
Understand	Summarize the design principles, fleshing out the definitions where needed, and correct any misconceptions or address any questions.
Remember	Have the students create their own "cheat sheet" of the four design principles that they can use as a future reference.

> **TIP:** Even if you mix and match the levels as needed, it's still useful to pinpoint the level(s) you're aiming for. For example, if you are teaching someone how to read electrical schematics, you may never need to get beyond Analyze, and if your goal is for learners to apply a concept, you need to make sure your learning design doesn't stop at Understand.

HOW PROFICIENT SHOULD YOUR LEARNER BE?

Another way to look at how much you think your learner should learn is to ask how *proficient* you want your learner to become. There are a number of scales that address this, but I like this one from Gloria Gery:

- Familiarization
- Comprehension
- Conscious Effort
- Conscious Action
- Proficiency
- Unconscious Competence

(Gery, 1991)

If we apply this scale to our CRAP example, it might look something like this:

Scale	A Way The Learner Might Show This
Familiarization	Be able to recognize or recall the design principles.
Comprehension	Be able to explain or describe the principles, or recognize examples if prompted.
Conscious Effort	Attempt to design something by consciously using the principles.
Conscious Action	Successfully design something by consciously using the principles.
Proficiency	Successfully design things using the principles without laborious referencing.
Unconscious Competence	Design using the principles without even thinking about it, or deliberately referencing the principles.

By the time you hit unconscious competence with something like the graphic design principles, you are doing things like seeing movie posters out of the corner of your eye and wincing at the misalignment of the text elements. You've fully automated the ideas, and no longer have to put a lot of conscious effort toward the tasks.

Generally it takes quite a bit of time and practice to develop unconscious competence. If you think back to learning how to drive, it probably was months and years before you no longer had to expend a lot of conscious effort on the task. Some of the unconscious driving competencies you might now have probably took years to develop.

It's more unusual to invert this scale, but it can happen. Language learning is an example. You probably have unconscious competence in a number of grammar rules (you do them right without thinking about it) that you couldn't consciously explain.

Another way to think of it is as an XY axis—how sophisticated or complex do you want their understanding to be, and what level of proficiency do you want to get them to?

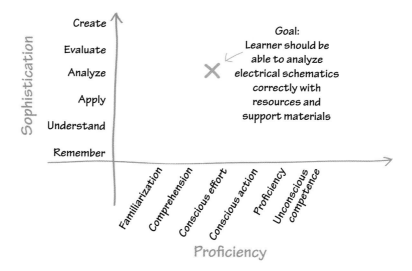

Not surprisingly, the higher you go on either scale, the more time, practice, and skills development you'll need to do. You absolutely cannot get past Conscious Action without a significant amount of practice distributed over time. You also can't get to the higher levels of sophistication without multiple examples, and without the opportunity to interact with those examples and get feedback.

A single exposure to the material will likely only familiarize the learner, or take them just a little bit further than that. If you are being asked to get learners to those higher levels, but being given only one point of contact with the learners (one class session or one e-learning course), it almost certainly can't be done.

COMMUNICATING LEARNING OBJECTIVES

One of the "rules" of training is that you tell the learners what the objectives are. When I first started taking instructional design classes, this was handed down as instructional design gospel ("Thou shalt inform learners of the learning objectives!").

That frequently manifests itself as a slide like this at the beginning of training presentations:

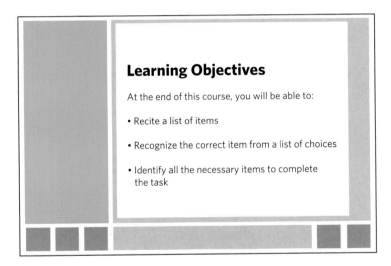

Ever seen one of those slides at the beginning of a training class? If not, maybe you blocked it out (I've certainly done that a time or two). If so, I can only hope the learning objectives were a bit better written than these, but why do we announce the learning objectives to our learners in the first place?

There are a few different reasons you might want to tell your learners what the objectives or goals are:

- To focus the learner's attention on the key points in the objectives
- To let learners know what to expect
- To let them know what level of performance they should be working towards

There are other reasons why you, as the learning designer, want to have clear learning objectives as well: You want a clear design direction so you know what you are trying to do (and just as importantly, what you are *not* trying to do), and you want to show a target or benchmark for assessing if you've succeeded at the end of the project. But again, these learning objectives are more for you as the designer than they are for the learner.

Will Thalheimer, an instructional design expert, has a taxonomy of different types of learning objectives:

Type	Purpose
Focusing Objective	A statement presented to learners before they encounter learning material, provided to help guide learner attention to the most important aspects of that learning material.
Performance Objective	A statement presented to learners before they encounter learning material, provided to help learners get a quick understanding of the competencies they will be expected to learn.
Instructional-Design Objective	A statement developed by and for instructional designers to guide the design and development of learning and instruction.
Instructional-Evaluation Objective	A statement developed by and for program evaluators (or instructional designers) to guide the evaluation of instruction.

(Thalheimer 2006)

New instructional designers frequently struggle with writing good learning objectives, partly because they are often being asked to cram all four of these functions into a single statement. That's like trying to pack all the gear for a family of four into a single carry-on bag—it's somewhere between difficult and impossible. It also means that learners are subjected to horrible instructional design jargon. That jargon can serve a purpose for the design team in making sure the learning objectives are precise, but it's just cruel to bludgeon your learners with it.

So, how might you think about each of these categories?

Type	Ask yourself	Example
Focusing Objective	Is there something I particularly want to focus the learner's attention on?	"JavaScript can be a useful tool, but it's not right for everything. In this module, you'll want to pay particular attention to how you'll decide if JavaScript is right for your project."
Performance Objective	What level of proficiency are you going to require from the user, and does the user need to know that's coming?	"Your mission, should you choose to accept, is to make recommendations back to the team about the five upcoming software projects, and whether JavaScript is the right tool to use. You will need to defend your decision to the team."
Instructional-Design Objective	What goal are you basing your design on?	Learner will be able to state whether or not JavaScript is an appropriate programming tool for a specific task and give a correct rationale for their decision.
Instructional-Evaluation Objective	A statement developed by and for program evaluators (or instructional designers) to guide the evaluation of instruction	"In scenarios judging the appropriateness of JavaScript, learners will have at least 80% decision-making accuracy, and be able to list from recall at least 75% of the criteria to justify their decisions."

And, for the record, just say no to learning-objective slides at the beginning of the course. If you want to communicate the objectives to the learner, use a challenge, a scenario, or a "your mission, should you choose to accept" message. There are a multitude of ways that *aren't* bullet points on a slide to accomplish the goals of focusing the learner's attention, and letting them know where they are headed.

DETERMINE THE GAP

Once you've set your learning objectives, you want to revisit the question of why learners aren't currently meeting those objectives. What are the gaps between their current situation and where you want them to be?

- **Knowledge gaps**—Sometimes it really is a matter of not having enough of the right information.
- **Skills gaps**—Someone could know what all the functions of all the controls in the cockpit of a 757 are, and you still wouldn't want them flying your plane unless they'd had sufficient practice. *Skills need to be developed over time.* Whenever knowing isn't enough, then skills also need to be developed.

- **Motivation or attitude gaps**—True or false: Most people don't exercise enough because they don't know how to do it. OK, that's probably false. Most people probably have enough knowledge, but struggle with motivation. Whenever knowledge and skills are present, but the person still isn't being successful, it's worth looking to see if there's an attitude or motivation gap.
- **Environment gaps**—Does the environment support the person in being able to succeed, or are there unnecessary roadblocks in the process or environment that keep them from being able to do the right thing? Do they have enough time and support to do that right thing?
- **Communication gaps**—Sometimes it isn't about knowledge, skills, or motivation, but about the directions being given. For example, a customer service representative might not be succeeding because of vague or conflicting directions (e.g., being told to make the customer happy while simultaneously reducing average call time). This isn't a learning problem as much as it is a communication or leadership problem.

So which comes first, the learning objective or the gap? The answer is both, pretty much. It's likely you are starting with some kind of need or challenge, and you are going to want to investigate both learning objectives and performance gaps. There are times when one will inform the other. For example, if you want to train people how to use the super-cool analysis feature in your software, you might have a learning objective about learners being able to run analysis reports. Subsequent gap analysis might tell you that learners do know the procedure for running the reports—they just don't know they can access their own data in the analysis. That would lead you to a very different learning objective.

HOW LONG IS THE TRIP?

When considering a learner's journey, think about how far your learner can really progress along the path.

Years ago I had a fairly blechy job teaching GMAT prep classes. The class met for an entire weekend (Friday night and all day Saturday and Sunday) to help prospective MBA students prepare to take the GMAT exam the following weekend. The students would take the short version of the GMAT on Friday night, and a full-length practice exam on Sunday.

It was a difficult job for a number of reasons (the pace, the last-minute info-cram format, the nasty windowless hotel meeting-room locations, the aura of exam stress in the room), but one of the biggest issues was whether or not we could actually help the students. The answer was mixed.

With a typical student, we stood a decent chance of improving their Quantitative (math, logic, problem-solving) scores, but we usually couldn't make much of a dent in their Verbal scores. I'll explain why in a moment, but stop for a second and think about why that might be the case.

Jeopardy theme music while you formulate a hypothesis...

Maybe it's obvious, but it came down to the specifics of what we could teach them. In the Quantitative section, we could teach them some quickie shortcuts for math problems, remind them of the geometry formulas they hadn't seen since their sophomore year of high school, and get them used to the wacky "data sufficiency" format that shows up on the test.

These skills were either information-based, based on activation of prior (albeit rusty) knowledge, or very quick to learn, and could therefore (in the case of the data-sufficiency format) could be brought to a reasonable level of mastery in a few hours (whether they retained those skills is another matter).

In the Verbal section, they needed skills like vocabulary, reading comprehension, complex analysis, and reasoning. As you might imagine, these are not skills you acquire in a weekend (try decades). There are very few quickie shortcuts that you can teach someone if the foundations of their language skills aren't there. This was amplified by the fact that right answers in the verbal section were relative answers ("Choose the best answer") instead of absolute ("Choose the correct answer")—they involved making judgment calls rather than calculating to find the one correct answer.

Some knowledge or skills can be acquired quickly, but others are slow, and take a long time to develop.

So how far down the path can a learner go?

I've had clients who have told me they want to teach problem-solving skills in a half-hour e-learning course.

Since problem-solving a skill that takes a looooong time to develop, I usually sigh quietly to myself, and then tell them a variant of the above story.

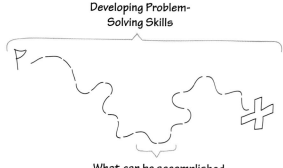

Developing Problem-
Solving Skills

What can be accomplished
in a single e-learning course

WHAT'S PACE LAYERING?

Stewart Brand is the author of a book called *How Buildings Learn: What Happens After They're Built*. In the book, he describes an idea called pace layering.

Basically, the idea is that some things change quickly (the actual contents of the room might change daily, the interior decorating might change in months to years), and some things will change more slowly (the space usage, the interior layout, the actual structure might change in years), and some things will change only very slowly (the structure, the foundation might change in years, decades, or centuries).

(Brand 1994)

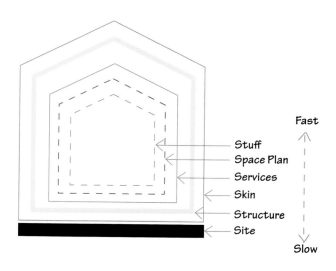

Stuff
Space Plan
Services
Skin
Structure
Site

Fast

Slow

Here's what Mr. Brand says (on The Long Now Foundation site) about the pace layering of cities and civilization:

The fast parts learn, propose, and absorb shocks; the slow parts remember, integrate, and constrain. The fast parts get all the attention. The slow parts have all the power.

This raises the question: What is the pace layering of learners? What can change quickly, and what changes more slowly?

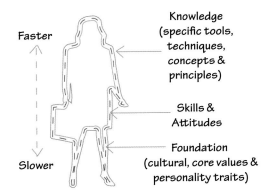

In the GMAT course I taught, we could—at best—rearrange some furniture (and hope that it stayed rearranged until they took the test the following week). We weren't going to really change anything like their verbal skills—those were part of the structure and foundation.

FAST OR SLOW?

If a particular learning point is fast, you might be able to get your learner all the way from beginning to end. If it's something very slow, like their problem-solving skills, you'll be lucky to inch them down the path.

Take a look at this example. Todd is a brand-new restaurant manager. He just got promoted, and needs to get his skills up to par as quickly as possible. Which of the skills that Todd needs to acquire are fast? Which are slow?

Todd, a brand new manager

Todd's new job requirements

Competencies	Fast or Slow?
Approve timesheets	Fast - - - - - - - - - - Slow
Communicate changes & updates to staff	Fast - - - - - - - - - - Slow
Create weekly schedules	Fast - - - - - - - - - - Slow
Design & implement creative seasonal promotions	Fast - - - - - - - - - - Slow
Ensure a respectful environment	Fast - - - - - - - - - - Slow
Forecast inventory requirements	Fast - - - - - - - - - - Slow
Minimize waste	Fast - - - - - - - - - - Slow
Perform monthly check of security & sprinkler systems	Fast - - - - - - - - - - Slow
Recognize & prevent harassment in the workplace	Fast - - - - - - - - - - Slow
Recognize & reward employees	Fast - - - - - - - - - - Slow
Resolve employee conflicts	Fast - - - - - - - - - - Slow
Train on proper procedures for safe alcohol sales	Fast - - - - - - - - - - Slow
Verify that tables are set properly	Fast - - - - - - - - - - Slow

Loosely speaking, approving timesheets, communicating changes, checking security and sprinkler systems, and verifying table settings are probably pretty fast skills. Creating weekly schedules, designing and implementing creative seasonal promotions, recognizing and preventing harassment, and training on safe alcohol sales are probably medium or a mixed sets of skills, and things like ensuring a respectful environment, forecasting inventory requirements, minimizing waste, recognizing and rewarding employees, and resolving employee conflicts are slow skills.

So what can you do with this? If you identify that something is a slow task, how do you approach it?

Find a few throw pillows. What are some easy, cheap ways to make an impact? It might be a model, a tool, a job aid, a checklist—something that's easy for your learners to implement right away, that will have an immediate impact. It won't change their world, but it might solve a small but pesky problem. Don't try to solve big problems with a throw pillow,
though. They may brighten the room, and be a cheap way to have an impact (and there's nothing wrong with that), but they aren't a substitute for the heavy lifting involved in real behavioral change.

Provide some sturdier pieces. Give them some more concrete material, but recognize that this is going to take more time; they will need to set it up, move it into place, get rid of the old piece, arrange their existing stuff in it, and get used to how it changes their current

patterns. Don't try to do that all at once; keep in mind that there are several steps and that all need to be supported, unless you want the unassembled items sitting in its box in the storage area indefinitely.

Recognize that you aren't going to change their structure. If they have some renovations already in place, you might move them along a little, or you can help them start some planning for future changes. This sounds easy, but actually, it's really hard, because it involves letting go of the deeply held belief that we can do major renovations in a short period of time. We can't—and it's a waste of resources to pretend we can. If we approach a learning design with the longer view in mind, acknowledging what we can and cannot accomplish, we can create better ways to help people, and ensure that there is a long-term plan.

Respect the foundation. The foundation is based on a learner's personal bedrock, which is comprised of elements like culture and personality. If your structural changes aren't going to sit well on the foundation, then you are better off changing your design, because it's really unlikely that the foundation is going anywhere.

DESIGNING FOR FAST AND SLOW

So how do you design for this? If something is fast, then that's pretty easy. You present the concept, make sure the learner has adequate opportunity to practice it, and reinforce it as necessary. Slow skills are really the problem. What do you do if it's a slow skill?

Let's take a look at the management skill of hiring the right people. That can be a pretty slow skill to develop. People who have been managers for 20 years can still be learning new things and getting better at this.

What can we do to help Todd improve his skills in this area?

Speed	Type	What You Can Do
Very Fast	Tools, checklists, specific procedures	Give Todd a checklist of hiring questions, and practice using and evaluating the answers. Have Todd use the list as a job aid while he's interviewing.
Moderate	Skills, practice, proficiency development	Practice scenarios and role-plays of hiring situations, spaced out over time with detailed feedback.
Slow	Higher-level conceptual and strategic skills, expert coaching, extensive practice	Have Todd receive expert coaching from an experienced manager. Also have him read and study deeper resources in the area and set personal development goals in this area.
Foundation	Evaluation, self-assessment, awareness	Have Todd assess his own skills, personality, and cultural biases, and how these things impact his abilities as a manager. Todd is unlikely to change those things, but learning to be aware of them can help him accept and work with them beneficially.

SUMMARY

- Use questions like "Why, why, no really, why?" and "What bad thing will happen if they don't know?" to uncover the real reason for learning.

- Define the problem before coming up with solutions, to ensure you are actually solving the real problem and not a problem you *don't* have.

- Use the two questions "Is this something the learner would actually do in the real world?" and "Can I tell when they've done it?" to make sure your learning objectives are useful and usable.

- Decide how sophisticated your learner's understanding needs to be, and how proficient they need to be, and then design accordingly.

- Recognize if you are teaching someone a fast or slow skill, and use strategies appropriate to developing that type of skill.

REFERENCES

Anderson, Lorin W. and David Krathwohl, eds. 2001. *A taxonomy for learning, teaching and assessing: A Revision of Bloom's Taxonomy of Educational Objectives, complete edition.* New York: Longman.

Bloom, Benjamin S. 1956. *Taxonomy of Educational Objectives, Handbook I: The Cognitive Domain.* New York: David McKay Co Inc.

Brand, Stewart. 1994. *How Buildings Learn: What Happens After They're Built.* New York: Viking.

Gery, Gloria. 1991. *Electronic Performance Support Systems: How and Why to Remake the Workplace through the Strategic Application of Technology.* Boston: Weingarten Publications.

Thalheimer, Will. 2006. New Taxonomy for Learning Objectives, *Will At Work Learning Blog,* June 1. http://www.willatworklearning.com/2006/06/new_taxonomy_fo.html.

HOW DO WE REMEMBER?

(In which we learn that memory is messy and that biking straight uphill isn't a good way to learn)

Memory is the foundation of learning, so let's take a few pages to talk about how learners actually learn and remember stuff. How does all that knowledge get in there on any given day? And how do we find and retrieve it when we need it?

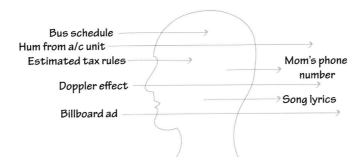

There's a lot we still don't know about the nature of memory, but we do have some ideas and models for how it works. First, we'll look at how we pay attention and encode information into memory. Second, we'll look at different types of memory.

MEMORY IN & OUT

Successful learning involves encoding and retrieval—memory in and memory out. Remembering is a necessary first step, but you need to be able to retrieve, manipulate, combine, and innovate with the information you remember.

Information in your brain doesn't just sit there like a wool sweater during summertime. When you put information in, it doesn't lie passively waiting to be taken out, but instead it interacts with other information. So your brain isn't *really* a closet.

In order for your brain to be like a closet, it would have to be a super-automated closet that reorganizes itself constantly, or one that's populated by some kind of closet elves who are continually moving and arranging things.

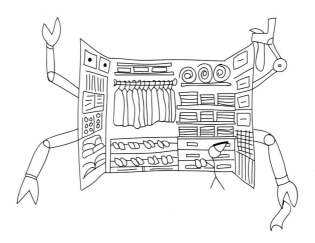

Also, anything you put in your closet automatically gets stored in multiple categories, so the blue socks your grandmother knitted for you would simultaneously (and magically) be put with things that are wool, things that are blue, socks, outfits that go with those socks, stuff from grandma, things that are starting to wear out, and so on.

What's more, the self-organizing closet has multiple, overlapping ways to keep track of things. So when you put away those blue socks in the "socks" drawer, the closet can retrieve them by looking on the "things that are wool" shelf, or on the "things that are blue" hanger.

Your brain is a dynamic, multi-faceted, constantly changing entity. Anything you retain from this book will change the physical structure of your brain by creating new connections and strengthening (or weakening) existing connections.

So what winds up sticking? We are bombarded with millions and millions of data points all day long. We can't possibly attend to—much less remember—all of them.

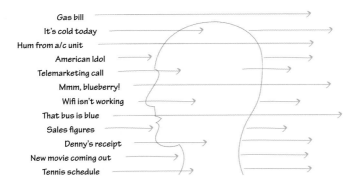

Fortunately, you have a series of filters and triggers that allows you to parse this information:

- **Sensory memory.** This type of memory is your first filter of everything you sense and perceive. If you choose to pay attention to something, it gets passed on to short-term memory.
- **Short-term memory.** This is the memory that allows you to hold on to ideas or thoughts long enough to take action. Most things get discarded out of short-term memory, but some things get encoded into long-term memory.
- **Long-term memory.** This is your closet, where you store information that you'll keep for a while.

Let's take a closer look at each of these.

SENSORY MEMORY

The first level of memory is sensory memory. Basically pretty much anything you sense is held momentarily in your sensory memory.

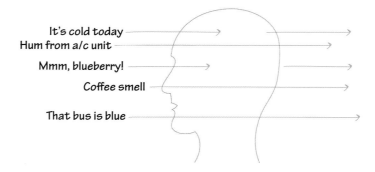

Most sensations keep right on going, unless there's something unusual or note-worthy about what you are sensing.

For example, stop right now and pay attention to all the noises you can hear. If you are indoors, you are likely hearing the hum of an air conditioning or heat-ing unit, or noise from appliances or computers. If you are outside, there will be environmental noises depending on your location.

Unless someone or something calls your attention to one of these, you probably weren't paying attention to those noises, and you were certainly not encoding those noises into your memory.

HABITUATION

Sensory memory isn't a big concern for learning designers, except for the phe-nomena of habituation. Habituation means getting used to a sensory stimulus, to the point that we no longer notice or respond to it.

Habituation is what allows you to stop noticing the annoying refrigerator buzz after you've been listening to it for a while, or when you stop even noticing that "check engine" light on the dashboard when it's been on for weeks.

If things are unpredictable, they can be harder to habituate to. For example, the horrible torment of a flickering fluorescent light persists long after you've stopped hearing the hum from the computer monitor, because the unpredict-able pattern of the flicker keeps calling our attention to it over and over and over...

Similarly, being stuck in traffic stays infuriating because it's rarely uniform (start... stop...start...little faster...STOP...go...go go ...Go...GOGOGOGO... *Stooop!*).

People can also habituate to things that we don't necessarily want them to. For example, when was the last time you paid much attention to the advertisements in the banner at the top of web pages? You've probably learned how to tune those out. Web designers refer to that as "banner blindness," and eye-tracking studies (Nielsen 2007) verify that people not only don't pay much attention to banner ads, they frequently don't look at them at all. (The same thing can happen with resource and reference material we provide for learners on websites and in e-learning courses!)

IMPLICATIONS FOR LEARNING DESIGN

Consistency can be useful. Consistency can be a useful tool to make things easier for your learner. For example, if you use the same basic format for each chapter of a technical manual, your learners get used to the format and don't have to expend mental energy repeatedly orienting themselves to the format; instead, they can focus on the *content* of the chapters.

Too much consistency is bad. However, too much consistency can lead to habituation in your learners. You want to vary your teaching methods and the way you present information. For example, if you are creating an e-learning program and you give the same type of feedback in the same location every single time, then learners are going to learn to ignore it, particularly if the feedback is the generic "Good Job!" kind. Another example of too much consistency is the "banner blindness" mentioned above.

Annoying variability is bad, too. While some variation is useful for keeping the learner's attention, meaningless differences are just irritating. For example, if you take that e-learning feedback box and have it randomly pop up in different areas of the screen, it will probably keep the learner from habituating to it as quickly, but it's also going to really annoy them. A better approach would be to have different feedback formats that are appropriate to the different types of content you are presenting, or to use a variety of different learning activities to keep things interesting. Variation can be a useful tool for maintaining attention, but it should be used in a deliberate and meaningful way.

The best way to know if something is too consistent is through user testing. Watch your learners interact with print or electronic materials, or pilot test a class—if your learners are inattentive or seem to obviously ignore resource materials, that's a clue that they've start to gloss past those elements.

SHORT-TERM OR WORKING MEMORY

Once something has attracted your attention, it moves into your short-term or working memory. If it succeeds in penetrating your short-term memory, it's probably something that:

- Is significant to you for some reason
- You are looking for
- You need to take action on
- Surprises or confounds your expectations

Working memory has a relatively short duration and limited capacity, but you use it pretty much constantly throughout the day.

WHAT DO YOU RETAIN?

For example, let's say you are deciding what to wear to work today. You glance at the weather (cool and rainy), and at your schedule (client meeting). You hold those two things in working memory while you check your closet. You also retrieve some information from long-term memory (the conference room is always hot; the black suit is at the cleaners because of that unfortunate guacamole stain).

New information in working memory	Pulled from long-term memory
Cool and rainy weather	Conference room is always hot
Client meeting	Black suit is at the cleaners

All this information gets processed together as you make the decision to wear layers.

Working memory will discard most pieces of information as soon as you're done with them, like the wifi password at the coffee shop, the number of the freeway exit you need to take, or the phone number that you recite over and over until you can get it dialed.

All of those types of information are the kind of thing that you might keep in working memory for the few seconds that you will need it. If it takes you longer, you might also keep it there via repetition.

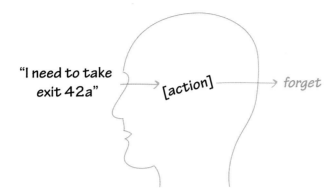

Repetition will refresh the information in working memory until you use it and stop repeating. If you repeat something long enough, you will eventually grind it into long-term memory, but that's not the most efficient method (we'll discuss better methods later). Some information will drop out more quickly if it doesn't have significance.

Let's take a look at the following three pieces of information you might hear in the morning news radio report.

Information: *The temperature is 12 degrees Celsius.*

Factors that influence retention:

- *Is it unusual? If it's significantly different than the weather for the last few days, it's more likely to catch your attention.*

- *Is it important to you? You'll retain it better if the weather affects your plans for the day.*

- *Is it a familiar format? If you ordinarily use Fahrenheit, you're unlikely to remember the Celsius temperature, because you won't know if it means you should wear your coat.*

If you do remember it for the length of the day, it's still unlikely you'll continue to remember it days or weeks later, unless there was something significant about the date (e.g., your brother's wedding day).

Information: *The Dow Jones industrial average is up 56 points, or 0.5 percent, to 11,781.*

Factors that influence retention: *The same issues apply. Does this contrast with previous days or expectations? Is this significant to you because you work with the financial markets, or are waiting to sell some stock?*

Information: *UConn Huskies lost to the Stanford Cardinals 71-59.*

Factors that influence retention: *You are likely to retain this information only if you follow US Women's college basketball, or if you know that this was the first game the UConn team had lost after setting the record for the most consecutive games won (89 in a row). If you don't have that context, you probably won't retain any part of that information.*

WHAT'S THE LIMIT?

How much can you hold in working memory? There is a fair amount of research on the limits of working memory, and there's a well-known statistic about 7±2 items in working memory, but the real answer is *it depends*. (Miller 1956)

In all likelihood, you can't repeat all the data from the previous table (the temperature, the Dow Jones numbers, and the sports scores) without going back and checking it again. The main reason you can't is because those numbers have no significance for you, beyond being an example in this book.

An additional reason would be the quantity of information—there were several discrete facts in that table (12°, Celsius, Dow Jones, 56 points, 0.5%, 11, 781, UConn Huskies, Stanford Cardinal, 71, 59). That's more pieces of individual information than most people can remember without some kind of memory aid or device.

Read this number, and then close your eyes and try to repeat it:

6 7 1 8

How'd you do? In all likelihood you did pretty well at retaining that briefly. Four discrete digits is usually well within the limits of working memory.

Now try this number:

934871625

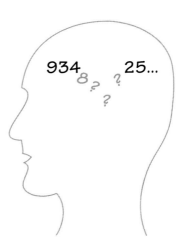

That one is a little harder, right? Maybe you were able to retain all nine digits, but if you dropped some digits they were likely to be somewhere in the middle of the string of numbers. That would be an example of primacy and recency effects, which suggest we are more likely to remember something at the beginning of a sequence or list (primacy) and also more likely to remember the most recent things, as at the end of a list (recency).

OK, now try this one:

100 500 800

That's a whole lot easier, right? It's the same number of digits, but it's *chunked*. Instead of remembering individual digits, you are remembering something like this:

[first three digits] + [next three digits] + [last three digits]

This is three chunks of information, rather than nine separate chunks of information.

Even easier is:

123456789

Because you already know how to count to nine, this is just one chunk of information for you:

[digits 1–9 in order]

Chunking can be based on things that are similar, sequential, or items that are in your long-term memory.

For example, try this number:

612 651 763 952

In all likelihood, this is too much information for you to retain in working memory, unless you live in the Minneapolis / St. Paul area, where these are the local telephone area codes.

WHAT DOES THIS MEAN FOR LEARNING DESIGN?

Who memorizes strings of numbers anymore? Doesn't everybody have a cell phone?

We are fortunate to have devices we can use to offload tedious details, and most people don't have any need to remember random strings of numbers (which is a good thing, because humans mostly suck at that particular task, while electronic devices are brilliant at it).

But using chunking in learning—whether it involves large numbers or large amounts of textual or perhaps even visual information—will help your learners manage their working memory, and help them understand where to focus their limited attention at any given point.

Let's say you are teaching somebody a procedure—for example, how to bake an apple pie. Take a look at this list of steps:

Mix together the flour and the salt.

Chill the butter and water.

Add the butter to the flour and cut it with a pastry blender until it resembles coarse crumbs.

Add enough water until the dough barely hangs together.

Cut the dough in half and make two balls.

Wrap the dough in plastic wrap and refrigerate.

Peel the apples.

Core and quarter the apples and cut into 1/4" slices.

Mix the apples with sugar, lemon juice, cinnamon, and a small amount of flour.

Roll out one of the pieces of pie dough into a circle slightly larger than your pie pan.

Fold the pie dough in half and lift it into the pie pan.

Press the dough into the pan.

Fill the pie dough with the apple mixture.

Roll the other piece of dough into a circle.

Place the dough on top of the pie and crimp the edges.

Cut steam holes in the top crust.

Bake the pie for 45 min in a 350° oven.

That's a lot of steps, right? A bit much for someone to process. If they know a lot about baking, they'll be able to parse that information in a way that makes sense, but if the learner doesn't have a lot of context for pie-making, then this list is likely to overwhelm them quickly.

There's no cue to tell them when to stop reading the new information for a moment, and process the existing information. There's also no higher-level organization for the material—it's just a long list of steps. Which is why you want to look for opportunities to chunk that information:

Prepare the dough

Mix together the flour and the salt.

Chill the butter and water.

Add the butter to the flour and cut it with a pastry blender until it resembles coarse crumbs.

Add enough water until the dough barely hangs together.

Cut the dough in half and make two balls.

Wrap the dough in plastic wrap and refrigerate.

Prepare the filling

Peel the apples.

Core and quarter the apples and cut into 1/4" slices.

Mix the apples with sugar, lemon juice, cinnamon, and a small amount of flour.

Assemble the pie

Roll out one of the pieces of pie dough into a circle slightly larger than your pie pan.

Fold the pie dough in half and lift it into the pie pan.

Press the dough into the pan.

Fill the pie dough with the apple mixture.

Roll the other piece of dough into a circle.

Place the dough on top of the pie and crimp the edges.

Bake the pie

Cut steam holes in the top crust.

Bake the pie for 45 min in a 350° oven.

Even just chunking the steps into four categories makes the whole procedure much easier for people to process and remember. Chunking isn't magically going to allow the learner to remember the whole recipe, but it will help them to focus on a single section at any one time, and the steps in an individual chunk are a more realistic quantity of information to hold in working memory.

Working memory acts as a gatekeeper for long-term memory, so if the initial information overloads working memory, it's unlikely to make the transition to long-term memory.

LONG-TERM MEMORY, OR IS IT IN YOUR CLOSET?

Ultimately, when we are teaching or learning something, what we really want is for the information to reach long-term memory—firmly situated in the closet, in a place where we can find it again easily.

WHERE DO YOU PUT IT?

Anything that you do remember becomes part of a series of associations—you don't learn anything in isolation.

For example, say you've just learned that the German word for *mustache* is *Schnurrbart*. Now, in all likelihood, you don't care about this information, and you will let it wash out of your short-term memory without a ripple.

But suppose there is some reason you need to retain this information (a German vocabulary test, a fascination with words that sound like sneezes, an interest in European facial hair trends). How will you encode it? Well, of course, that depends on the shape of your closet, and the types of shelves that you have for that information. Fortunately, you don't have to choose a single association—you can store this item on all of those shelves simultaneously.

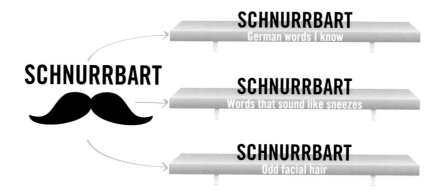

More (and better) associations will make it easier to retrieve the information. If you don't have a good shelving system for this word, you can create a mnemonic for it (tell yourself a story about sitting across from a German man with an elaborate mustache while riding the Bay Area Rapid Transit (BART) system, for example).

If you already speak German, you probably wouldn't need a mnemonic, as you'd already have a much more sophisticated shelving system for this word, involving the root meanings of the parts of the word ("bart" means beard in German), or other associations.

Your ability to retrieve information depends on the condition and contents of the shelves it's stored on in your mental closet.

MULTIPLE SHELVES

The more ways you have to find a piece of information, the easier it is to retrieve, so an item that goes on only one or two shelves is going to be harder to retrieve than an item that goes on many shelves.

For example, let's take two five-digit numbers: My mother's zip code and the salary offer I had for my first job after graduate school.

I don't have many shelves for the first number:

MY MOTHER'S ZIPCODE
Zipcodes I know

I don't use this number very often, and I don't have very many ways to access the information (I either remember it or I don't). In fact, these days I don't actually remember it, and have to get it from one of the external resources I use to supplement my memory (like an address book or a contact file on my phone). Basically, I have only one place to look for that number, and if that doesn't work, I don't have any other way to retrieve that information.

The salary offer, however, was a number with a lot more significance (sorry, Mom), and could be put on quite a few more shelves.

SALARY OFFER
What I'd like to earn

SALARY OFFER
What I thought other people earned

SALARY OFFER
What I earn now

SALARY OFFER
What I was earning before

As a result, I have multiple ways to access that information. I know it was almost twice what I was making before I went to graduate school, it was 10% less than a friend of mine made with the same degree (she was a much better negotiator), and I know how it compares to my current salary.

The more shelves you can put an item on, the more likely that you'll be able to retrieve it in the future. This is the problem with pure memorization tasks, such as flash cards—things you've learned that way tend to be on only one shelf (the "things you've memorized" shelf), which makes them harder to retrieve.

POORLY CONSTRUCTED SHELVES

Some of my shelves are pretty weak, and allow information to slip through. For example, I was trying to learn some Japanese before a trip a few years ago. Instead of a sturdy wooden shelf, my shelf for Japanese vocabulary was more like a rickety wire rack—I would carefully balance a few words and phrases there, but they'd frequently slip through, and I wouldn't find them when I went back to retrieve something.

Part of the reason my shelf for Japanese was so rickety was because I had so little context for Japanese. If I was trying to learn Spanish, I would have a sturdier shelf for that language despite being a novice it. My Spanish shelf would be strengthened by all the context I have for Spanish (things like similar Latin roots to some words in English, a close relationship to Italian, which I do know a little, and years of watching Spanish language vocabulary cartoons on Sesame Street as a child).

CROWDED SHELVES

A shelf that is crowded may not be specific enough. That can happen when you have a lot of information but not a very sophisticated structure for organizing that information. It makes it much more difficult to retrieve items accurately.

For example, my shelf for jazz music is pretty crowded—not because I know a lot about jazz (I don't), but rather because everything I do know about jazz— a specific artist name, that one piece that always makes me smile, the time period in which a certain style of jazz was born—all pretty much gets crammed on a single shelf labeled "Jazz." This means I have a really hard time retrieving specific information about jazz.

My shelves for '80s popular music, on the other hand, are embarrassingly well-developed. There are shelves for different genres, for American groups, British groups, hair bands, Americana, MTV, music videos, stuff I owned on LP, stuff I owned on cassette, bands I saw in concert, and so on (too bad you can't just deliberately choose to "unlearn" things).

UNINTENDED SHELVES

Sometimes associations are unintended. For example, a few years ago I was in Washington DC, staying a few blocks away from the Fannie Mae building while the mortgage association was being heavily discussed in the news. There was a lush bed of lavender plants in front of the building, and you couldn't walk by without smelling lavender.

Now, the Federal National Mortgage Association is forever on my lavender shelf (and vice versa).

This happens far more often than we realize. Our brain creates numerous associations that we may or may not be aware of, utilizing all our senses (sight, sound, touch, taste, and smell).

While these associations are somewhat random, they are still part of the associations we use to retrieve information. Let's take a look at how those associations can actually be used.

IN-CONTEXT LEARNING

Pop quiz: You're taking a class at the local university and have an in-class exam the next week. Where is the best place to study for a test?

A. Outside under a tree in peaceful sunshine
B. In your grey windowless classroom with a noisy air conditioning system
C. In a quiet, well-lit library
D. In a noisy coffee shop

The answer may be surprising: it's B, the grey windowless classroom. Yes, the one with the noisy air conditioning system. Why? Because the environment in which you study will become part of your association with the material you are studying. When possible, you want to encode the information in the same type of environment where you will also be retrieving that information.

The same is true for information that needs to be retrieved in a particular context, such as on the job. The further the learning is from the context of use, the fewer shelves are being utilized to store the information.

The context of the classroom is only helping you remember if you need to retrieve that information in a classroom. But we learn all sorts of information in classrooms that we need to apply later. Topics like plumbing and journalism and geology and hazardous materials handling are all taught in environments that are very different from the environments where those subjects will be used.

We have a tendency to hold classes in bare rooms far away from the place that use is going to happen, and that is a disservice to learners.

Deep down, we know this is true. Whenever lives are at stake, training almost always involves in-context learning. Even if the context is simulated—for the safety of the students or those around them—it's a rich, realistic context. Examples of in-context learning include flight simulators, teaching hospitals, and actual driving practice during driver's education.

If possible, you want to encode the information in the same type of environment where you will also be retrieving that information.

Isn't it inconceivable that drivers' education wouldn't involve actually road time? We wouldn't ever think someone could be a safe driver until they had actual experience driving in real traffic. Eventually simulators may be good enough and cheap enough to replace road practice, but for now, we take it for granted that learning to drive involves practice in the real context.

So why is out-of-context training acceptable in other circumstances? Frequently, it's a matter of convenience or cost or practicality. These can be very real constraints. For example, it might be nice to teach a server administration class in your actual server room, but you just can't get 30 people into a room the size of a large closet.

When practical constraints require that the learning can't happen in the physical space, there are still ways to increase the context. For example, if the class is about the physical setup of computer servers, it should involve hands-on contact with the equipment, even if it can't take place in the server room.

Many times, though, learning happens in an out-of-context environment like a bare, featureless classroom because of habit, tradition, or lack of awareness.

There are a variety of ways to make learning more in-context, despite practical constraints.

Think about ways you might improve or increase the context for learning experiences in the following scenarios:

Scenario 1: You need to teach consumers about the features of a new cell phone.

How would you make this a high-context experience? Consider how you might do it before reading the answer below.

> **Some possible design solutions** → Ideally, the learner would be interacting with those features on the actual phone as part of the learning experience, and would be trying them out. Additionally, anything that could be done to make the features part of actual use scenarios tailored to the audience would enhance context. So the learning experience would be real tasks that someone would do (texting a friend, entering a work contact), rather than just a guided tour of the features.

Scenario 2: You've been given the task of teaching college students how to make nutritionally balanced meals. What can you do to increase the context for this learning experience?

Some possible design solutions ➔ The learning experience should match the final setting as much as possible, which could mean operating in a cruddy dorm kitchen, using cheap cooking equipment from the local chain store, and reflecting the actual food scenarios. Another option would be to use photos of actual student refrigerators and challenge your learners to identify ways to make a healthy meal from the contents.

Scenario 3: You are creating a course to teach fast-food restaurant managers how to give employees constructive feedback. How would you make this learning experience high context?

Some possible design solutions ➔ Consider in what setting the feedback would take place, and use role-playing to practice. You could have managers create triggers for themselves by doing a mental tour of the restaurant, and thinking about what behaviors they would praise at each station. They could create a checklist for themselves of what to look for, where to look for it, and what to do if they see it.

EMOTIONAL CONTEXT

One of the most difficult types of context to create for learning situations is emotional context.

Let's take the employee feedback example. Let's say you are in a class with other students, and you are learning the principles of giving difficult feedback. What's the mood like in the classroom? Everybody is probably calm, nobody is upset. People are being serious and thoughtful as befits a classroom environment.

Now, think about the environment when you have to use what you learned. There's a good chance you are nervous, maybe anxious. The person you are talking to is probably unhappy, upset, or even hostile.

So, I wanted to talk to you about these areas for potential improvement...

How It's Supposed to Go

Sure, I can see how that could really help...

So, I had a few things...mostly you do a great job...but...well, there are a few things we should discuss...

How It Actually Goes

Why is this the first time I'm hearing about this?! Why didn't you bring it up before???

In this instance, the emotional context while learning about the material and then while applying it are very different. Many things seem reasonable when we are learning about them, like, when dealing with a hostile employee, staying calm, using "I" statements, validating the other person's point of view, etc.

But then you are actually confronted with a really angry person, and all that good advice flies out of your head, and fight-or-flight reactions surge to the front and you couldn't compose a validating "I" statement if your life depended on it.

We may be prepared with the knowledge and the protocols, but unable to implement them in the unfamiliar emotional context.

During Learning

During Application

I believe this is why a lot of learning fails. Have you ever said to yourself "I *knew* the right thing to do, but..." The difference between knowing and doing can be a huge gap when the context of encoding and the context of retrieval are significantly different.

There are many things we learn where the emotional context for use is drastically different than the emotional context for learning. We can be trying to retrieve the information when we are in a stressed or otherwise heightened emotional state:

Stressful or emotionally heightened circumstances can cause us to rely less on our intellectual knowledge and more on our automatic responses. This makes it more difficult to transfer something learned in a placid emotional context to a fraught emotional context.

So how can you create proper and effective emotional contexts? There are several ways:

Use role-playing. Even though we know it's not real, role-playing can be an effective way to create the feel of the emotional context, especially if you have someone effective playing the part. Even though it won't be exactly the same, just having practiced saying the words out loud make them easier to recall in real-life situations.

Create pressure. Even if the pressure is different, sometimes adding elements of similar pressure can create similar feelings. For example, a tight time limit on responses can create time pressure, which can approximate the emotional context of other types of pressure.

Invest in high-quality stories, acting, and performance. If it's critical material, get good actors or voice actors, and establish a strong emotional setup.

ENCODING FOR RETRIEVAL, OR HOW WILL IT NEED TO BE USED?

One of the things you will also want to consider is how the information will need to be used when it's retrieved. Will the learners only need to recognize the information, will they need to recall it outright, or will they need to be able to use it to actually do something?

That's the option I need.

Recognize?

The options are as follows...

Recall?

If we change out the options offered, we'll increase sales by 5%.

Integrate and Use?

You want the information encoding to align with assessment and use.

If someone is just going to need to recognize the right answer, then recognition activities are good ways to learn and practice. If someone needs to recall something unprompted, then they will need to learn and practice by recalling, not just by recognizing.

Which question is easier to answer?

Question 1: The French word for pool is _____. *(fill in the blank)*

Question 2: The French word for pool is:

a) Roman   b) Piscine   c) Plage   d) Plume

The second question is easier, right? *Recognizing* the right answer from a set of options almost always involves less effort than *recalling* the answer.

Learning experiences frequently rely heavily on recognition activities such as multiple-choice questions. This is particularly true in e-learning, where the computer is used to evaluate the correctness of student answers. This is primarily a practical choice. Recognition activities are easier to grade—computers can do it for us. Recall activities usually require a person to evaluate.

A PRACTICAL EXAMPLE

Look at the examples on the facing page for practicing and assessing a learner's CPR proficiency. Are they good examples? Why or why not? Stop and decide which one is the best before reading further.

CPR requires *recall*—remembering the right steps and how to do them properly. None of the activities you see here are really recall activities. They are mostly recognition activities.

The simulation comes the closest, but you can still simply guess. Also, the context is problematic—it's very different to click on the virtual chest of a patient on a computer screen rather than to apply pressure to an actual patient.

These learning activities might be *part* of a good learning experience, but they don't actually allow the learner to practice recalling the steps in the way that they will need to in a real-life situation.

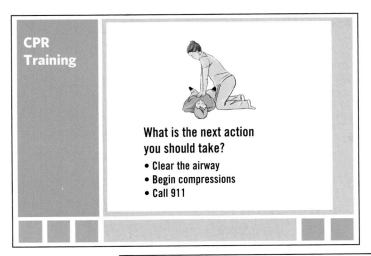

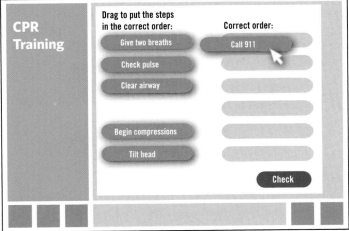

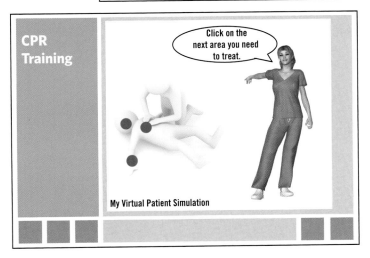

So how can you create learning activities that are a better match for the real-world application?

- Ensure that the practice involves recall or application.

Do you know all the steps?

Test yourself:

Recall Activity

Put the steps in the right order:

Give two breaths _____

Check pulse _____

Clear airway _____

Call 911 _____

Begin compressions _____

Tilt head _____

Recognition Activity

- Ensure that the practice and assessment are high-context.

- Use job aids to change something from a recall to a recognition task. Job aids change the task from "recall the steps" to "follow these steps," reducing the need to rely on memory. If you do use job aids, give your learners a chance to practice with the job aid as part of the learning. We'll talk more about this in later chapters.

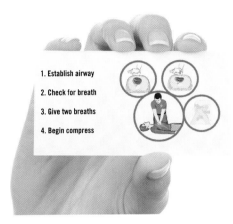

In the end, the practice needs to match the eventual use. If the learner just needs enough familiarity to recognize the right option, then practicing with recognition activities will be sufficient. If the learner needs to recall the material, or to do something more sophisticated like integrate the material, then the practice activities need to reflect that eventual use.

REAL VS PERCEIVED KNOWLEDGE

Frequently we think we know something because we recognize it—we *think* we know more than we actually *do* know.

What I think I know:

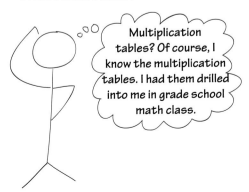

What I actually know:

So my conviction that I know the multiplication tables is a little suspect. I apparently know some parts of the multiplication tables, and I know some strategies for extending that knowledge (which is fortunate, because I would apparently be multiplication-illiterate without those strategies).

Let's say you are studying for an exam. You are chewing your pencil, reading your textbook, and nodding—it all looks pretty familiar. You've been studying like that for a while, and you are feeling pretty good about the whole thing.

Then you get to class, and you see this:

Recognition knowledge—the kind that might have gotten you through a multiple-choice test—is suddenly inadequate in the face of a mostly blank sheet of paper.

If you want to eventually retrieve information from your memory, you need to *practice* retrieving it when you study. (Karpicke 2011)

When you are teaching, you need to make sure that your learning activities allow your learners to practice in the same way that they will need to perform.

TYPES OF MEMORY

So far, we've been talking generally about the way a stimulus gets encoded into long-term memory, but there isn't just one general type of memory. There are actually several different types of memory that are encoded and retrieved in distinct ways. Some types of memory will be more appropriate to focus on depending on your subject matter, and learning design can often benefit from taking advantage of different types of memory.

There's a well-known story in psychology about an amnesia patient who did not have the ability to form new explicit memories. Her doctor had to reintroduce himself to her every time they met, because she couldn't remember him from day to day.

One day, as an experiment, the doctor hid a small sharp object in his hand when he shook the patient's hand in greeting.

When he followed up with her later, she had no explicit memory of meeting him, and needed to be introduced to him yet again, but when he offered his hand, she didn't want to shake it, even though, when asked, she couldn't give any reason for her reluctance.

This suggests that memories are processed in different ways, and that people are not consciously aware of all their memories.

What you know you know—The overlapping area (above) is your explicit memory. You know it and you know you know it, and can talk about it, if needed.

What you don't know you know—The rest of the blue area is your *tacit* memory. You know it, but couldn't describe it in any detail, or talk about it in a meaningful way. Sometimes it is things you forgot you knew, and other times it is things that are encoded in memory without your conscious awareness. You don't need to be an amnesiac to have tacit knowledge.

What you only *think* you know—The yellow area is made up of things you only think you know, but when you try to use those bits, your knowledge is incomplete or reconstructed incorrectly. Everybody has this—it's part of the messy human cognition process.

Within these categories, there are many different types of memory. While we are still very much in the process of understanding how different types of memory work in the brain, some of the types of memory include:

- **Declarative or semantic memory.** This is stuff you can talk about—facts, principles or ideas, like WWII ending in 1945, or your zip code.
- **Episodic memory.** This is also a form of declarative memory, but it's specific to stories or recollections from your own experience, like what happened at your graduation, or when you started your first job.
- **Conditioned memory.** Like Pavlov's dog, we all have conditioned reactions to certain triggers, whether we realize it or not, like when a pet gets excited about the sound of the can opener which precedes getting fed.
- **Procedural memory.** This is memory for how to perform procedures, like driving a car or playing the piano.
- **Flashbulb memories.** We seem to have a special type of memory for highly emotionally charged events, like national catastrophes.

Each of the different types of memory has different characteristics and different applications.

DECLARATIVE OR SEMANTIC MEMORY

Declarative memory is mostly the stuff you know you know, and can state explicitly, like facts, principles, or ideas.

Sometimes it's stuff you put into your closet deliberately (multiplication tables, for example), and sometimes it's material that you know despite not having made any conscious effort to retain (everything I know about Britney Spears, for example).

EPISODIC MEMORY

Episodic memory is also a form of declarative memory, in that you can talk about it, but it's related to specific events or experiences you've had.

For example, you may be able to remember a lot of things about dogs—they are pets, they have four legs, they are furry, they eat dog food, Scooby-doo is a dog, etc.

But you also probably have episodic memories about specific dogs that you've known—your childhood dog, the neighbor's dog, or the scary dog that followed you to school when you were little.

STORYTELLING

Episodic memory refers specifically to our memory for things that have happened to us in our lives, but even when a particular story didn't happen to us personally, we seem to have a singular ability to remember stories.

At the beginning of their book *Made to Stick*, Chip and Dan Heath compare two passages. The first is an urban legend (a man meets a woman in a bar and wakes up later in a bathtub full of ice with a kidney missing) and the second is a paragraph about the return-on-investment rationale for non-profit organizations (or something like that).

A few years after reading the book, I can still remember several salient details from the urban legend and nothing at all about the second passage. There are multiple reasons why that's the case, but a big part of it is because the first passage is a *story*.

There are a few reasons why stories seem to stick in our memories:

We have a framework for stories. There's a common framework for stories that we've all learned from the first stories we heard in childhood. Whether we realize it or not, in each culture there are common elements that we expect to hear when someone tells us a story. There's a beginning, middle, and end. There's the setup, the introduction of the players, and the environment. There's The Point of the story, which is usually pretty easy to recognize when it comes along. These are all shelves in our "how storytelling works" closet that give us places to store the information as we encounter it.

Stories are sequential. If I tell you 10 random facts about tennis, you need to expend mental energy trying to organize those facts somehow, possibly grouping like items or using some other strategy. If I tell you the story of a particularly gripping tennis match with 10 significant events, then the sequence of events provides a lot of the organization for you. Additionally, there's an internal logic to events in stories (logically, dropping the carton of eggs can't happen *before* the trip to the grocery store in the story of having a bad day).

Stories have characters. We have a lot of shelves to store information about people, their personalities, and their characteristics. If the story is about people we know, then we have all that background information to make remembering easier, and we have expectations about how they will behave. And if the character confounds your expectations by acting in a way that conflicts with your assumptions, that is surprising and novel and subsequently more memorable.

Which of the following would you be more interested in learning more about?

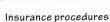

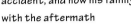

Insurance procedures

A story about Jim, a teen who was injured in a car accident, and how his family dealt with the aftermath

Steps to query a database

A story about Carla, the new employee who is the only one left in the office when the vice president calls down with an emergency request for updated reports

Human resources hiring best practices

A story about Marco, the replacement hiring manager in a company currently being sued for discriminatory hiring practices

CONDITIONED MEMORY

So you are cruising down the highway, and you glance in your rear view mirror and see a police car right behind you. Pop quiz—what do you do?

You slow down, right? Even if it becomes immediately apparent that the cop isn't the least bit interested in you, you've already dropped your speed, even if you weren't speeding in the first place.

What's happening there? Probably you didn't think to yourself, "Hmm, there seems to be a police officer behind me. Perhaps I should reduce my speed! I think I'll just gently let up on the gas pedal...easy does it..."

No, it was probably something more like, "WHOA!!" and you stomped your foot on the brake.

You see the stimulus of the police car, and you have what is a pretty much automatic reaction to what you see. This is what is referred to as a *conditioned response*.

Our conditioned responses are a form of implicit memory. Somewhere, stored in a part of your brain that you don't necessarily have explicit access to, there's a formula like this:

Everyone has reactions ingrained in their memory. Many are useful reactions acquired either through unconscious association or through deliberate practice:

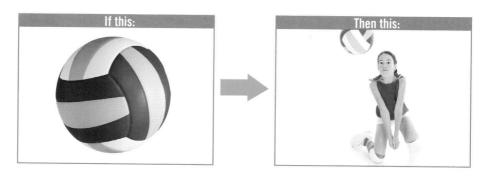

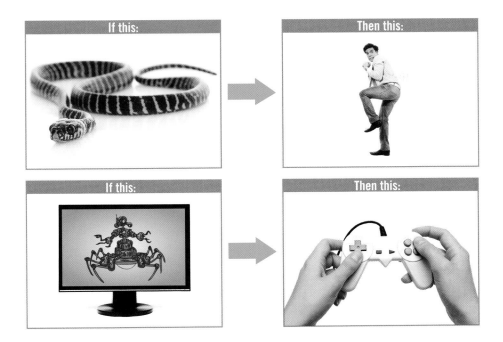

Some actions didn't need much effort to encode (like recoiling from a snake). We acquire others deliberately, through practice and repetition.

PROCEDURAL MEMORY

Procedural memory is our memory for how to *do* things. Specifically, it's our memory for how to do things that require a step-by-step process.

Some of the procedures you know are consciously learned, and you can explicitly state each step, but a lot of procedural memory is implicit.

Have you ever:

- Known how to get somewhere, but been unable to give somebody directions to that place?
- Gotten all the way home on your daily drive from work and realized that you have no memory of the drive itself?
- Been unable to remember a phone number or a PIN without tapping it out on the actual keypad?
- Thought you explained all the steps for a task to someone and then realized after it didn't work that you had neglected to mention some crucial details?

Those are all examples of utilizing something in your unconscious procedural memory. You use repeated practice of a procedure to make it become an unconscious habit. This is pretty important because it frees up your conscious attention to do other things.

Do you remember when you were first learning to drive? Everything required effort and attention.

Even if you were a pretty good student driver, you were still a bad driver, because you had to pay so much attention to everything, until you acquired enough practice to start automating some of the steps. Attention is a finite resource, and new drivers spread it pretty thin. Fortunately they start automating functions pretty quickly, and can then allocate a bigger chunk of their attention to things like not crashing, or avoiding pedestrians.

When you've been driving for a while, you (presumably) have freed up a lot of your attention for other things besides the basic mechanics of driving, so you can then, for example, change the radio station while switching lanes, and sing along at the same time. Of course, you may still be a bad driver years later, but that's probably due to other issues.

Automated procedural memory is related to the idea of **muscle memory** which, despite the name, is still really a brain function. Muscle memory refers to your procedural memory for certain tasks where you have learned something through practice so well that you don't have to put *any* noticeable conscious effort toward the task.

You get muscle memory through practice, and more practice, and even more practice (a process called *overlearning*). The biggest benefit of this is that you can perform the task without using up your conscious brain resources, freeing up those resources for other things.

It's frequently difficult to talk to others about these kinds of tasks, because you didn't learn them in a verbal, explicit way. You may know how to exactly adjust your golf swing to account for wind conditions, but you may not be able to explain it clearly to someone else. You can probably explain the overall motions, but not the subtleties (timing, how much pressure, the feel when you know it's correct).

FLASHBULB MEMORY

A few years ago, a freeway bridge near my home collapsed during rush hour, causing the death of about a dozen people, and injuring over a hundred more. It was widely reported in the national media at the time.

I vividly remember where I was when I heard about it. I was in a meeting room at the office working on a conference proposal. The lights were dim, and one of the cleaning people came in and told me about the bridge. I remember what chair I was sitting in, all the details of the proposal I was working on, and which website I used to get more information about the incident.

This type of vivid memory for emotionally charged events is call **flashbulb memory**. It's common for people to be able to recollect exactly where they were when they heard about the September 11th terrorist attacks, for example.

So what is the cause of this type of memory, and what does it have to do with learning? (Not that staging a major newsworthy event is a practical way to encourage retention.)

Many believe that flashbulb memory developed as part of our brain's attempt to keep us alive.

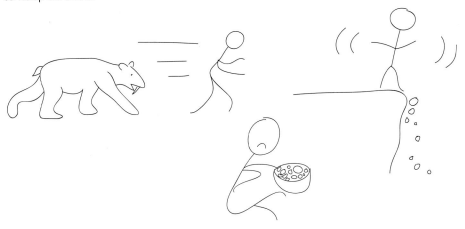

If you survive a death-defying encounter, **you want to remember how you did it**. Remembering how you got away from the bear is a much higher survival priority than remembering where you left that rock. You can forget all sorts of day-to-day things without dying, but if you bump into a bear a second time, forgetting key information from your first encounter may get you killed.

Things you can forget and not die

Things that can kill you

Ordinarily, it takes time, effort, and repetition to get things into your long-term memory, but in emotionally charged circumstances, the floodgates open and take in everything in the timeframe around the event. Sometimes it seems like time stands still.

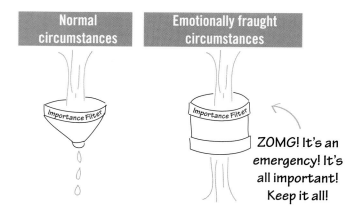

One theory about why time seems to slow in an emergency is that you just remember so much more from those harrowing seconds than you do from the same amount of time in a normal circumstance. (Stetson 2007)

Even though I have never been personally harmed or threatened by an event like a bridge collapse or a terrorist attack, the heightened emotional charge of just hearing about the event seems to be enough to enhance my memory.

Even in less dire circumstances, emotion seems to have an impact on how much we remember. We will revisit this idea in later chapters and look at specific methods for using emotion to enhance retention.

REPETITION AND MEMORY

With a few exceptions, learning almost always requires practice and repetition. For some reason, these are some of the most neglected aspects of learning design. Ever heard a variation on this conversation?

First supervisor: The staff is still throwing away the empty cartridges.

Second supervisor: But I *know* we told them not to. See, it's the third bullet point on slide 22 of the training presentation.

When you learn something new, connections are formed between neurons in your brain.

Like the paths that gradually develop when people repeatedly walk over the same ground, the connections that form in the brain are strengthened and reinforced whenever a learner re-encounters the material.

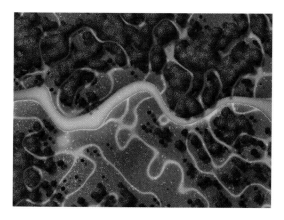

Connections that are reinforced become stronger and more durable. And, like a path that sees dwindling traffic, connections that aren't reinforced will usually fade or become irretrievable. Repetition and practice are necessary to success- fully retain most learning for the long term.

Also, it's important for a learning designer to figure out how to have reinforce- ment without resorting to monotonous repetition. We know that multiple exposures to an idea improve the likelihood that the idea will be retained (well and good). BUT (and this is a big but) habituation tells us that people also tune out repetitive, unchanging things.

In the later design chapters, we look at how to reinforce an idea while avoiding tedious repetition.

MEMORIZATION: THE BLUNT FORCE SOLUTION

So if repetition is so critical, why is memorizing stuff such a pain in the ass? Should we just get tough and use lots and lots or repetition to grind that information into people's heads?

When I was in college, I took an architecture class. The professor was explaining about early church buildings. She explained the people building the churches wanted to make the buildings as tall as possible, because they believed high ceilings enhanced churchgoers' religious feeling.

There were two different ways, the professor said, to make a building really tall: Use clever engineering to support the walls, or just make the walls really thick.

Using pure memorization to grind something into a learner's brain is the equivalent of building really thick walls—yes, it works, but it takes a lot of resources, and it's a clunky solution.

> I will not just repeat things over and over.
> I will not just repeat things over and over.
>
> I will not just repeat things over and over.
> I will not just repeat things over and over.
>
> I will not just repeat things over and over.
> I will not just repeat things over and over.
>
> I will not just repeat things over and over.
> I will not just repeat things over and over.
>
> I will not just repeat things over and over.
> I will not just repeat things over and over.

The biggest problem with memorization through repetition is that it frequently puts the information on just one shelf:

PIECES OF INFORMATION
Stuff I memorized

When you learn something by using it in context, you put it on multiple shelves, and learn how to use that information in multiple contexts.

So basically, if you repeat something over and over, eventually you will wear a groove into your long-term memory, but there are some limitations to that approach.

- It's only on one shelf (basically the "stuff I memorized" shelf), which gives you only one place to look when you are trying to retrieve the information.
- You don't have experience using it in multiple contexts, so it's more difficult to take that information and transfer it to a variety of situations.
- You likely have sequential rather than random access to the information. If you learn something in a memorized sequence, then the context for that information is in that sequence, and your ability to retrieve it is also in that sequence. You probably have to tick through the list every time you need to retrieve something, which is much slower than being able to get directly to that item.

SUMMARY

- Memory relies on encoding and retrieval, so learning designers need to think about how the material gets into long-term memory, and also what the learner can do to retrieve it later.

- Learners are besieged with a constant flow of input, and things need to be significant to the learner to attract their attention.

- People habituate to monotonous stimuli, so learning design needs to not fall into a repetitive drone.

- Working memory has its limits, and it's easy to overwhelm a new learner. Limit or chunk the flow of new information to make it more manageable.

- People hold items in working memory only as long as they need them for some purpose. Once that purpose is satisfied, they frequently forget the items. Asking your learners to do something with the information causes them to retain it longer and increases the likelihood that that information will be encoded into long-term memory.

- The organization of long-term memory has an impact on a learner's ability to retrieve material. The material will be easier to retrieve if it is grounded in a rich context and accessible in multiple ways (i.e., on multiple shelves).

- Matching the emotional context of learning to the emotional context of retrieval improves the likelihood that the learner will be able to successfully use the material.

- Storytelling leverages an existing mental framework, and therefore information given in story forms can be easier to retain than other types.

- Repetition and memorization will work to encode information into long-term memory, but it's a limited strategy. This process can be tedious for learners and doesn't provide very many pathways for retrieval.

- There are many different types of memory, and utilizing multiple types can improve the likelihood material is retained.

REFERENCES

Memory. 2011. In *Encyclopædia Britannica*. Retrieved from http://www.britannica.com/EBchecked/topic/374487/memory

Feinstein, Justin S., Melissa C. Duffa, and Daniel Tranel. 2010. Sustained experience of emotion after loss of memory in patients with amnesia. *PNAS* 107(17): 7674-7679.

Heath, Chip and Dan Heath. 2007. *Made to Stick: Why Some Ideas Survive and Others Die*. New York: Random House.

Karpicke, Jeffrey D., and Janelle R. Blunt. 2011. Retrieval Practice Produces More Learning than Elaborative Studying with Concept Mapping, *Science:* DOI: 10.1126/science.1199327, 772-775.

Kensinger, Elizabeth A. 2007. Negative Emotion Enhances Memory Accuracy–Behavioral and Neuroimaging Evidence. *Current Directions in Psychological Science* 16(4): 213-218.

Miller, George A. 1956. The magical number seven, plus or minus two: some limits on our capacity for processing information. *Psychological Review* 63(2): 81–97.

Nielsen, Jakob. 2007. Banner Blindness: Old and New Findings. *Alertbox,* August 20, http://www.useit.com/alertbox/banner-blindness.html.

Stetson, C., M. P. Fiesta, and D. M. Eagleman. 2007. Does Time Really Slow Down during a Frightening Event? *PLoS ONE* 2(12): e1295.

HOW DO YOU GET THEIR ATTENTION?

(In which we learn how to talk to the elephant)

IF THEY'RE NOT PAYING ATTENTION...

Do you remember the *Ooo – shiny!* learner?

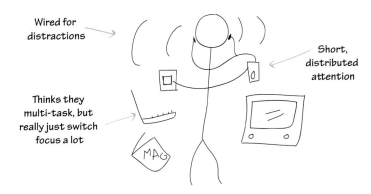

Wired for distractions

Short, distributed attention

Thinks they multi-task, but really just switch focus a lot

MAG

In our current world of 24-hour-a-day distractions, this is pretty much everybody; we all have an excess of things that try to command our time and attention. And attention is pretty critical, right? If your learners aren't paying attention, then it doesn't matter what kind of learning experience you've created—they aren't getting much from it.

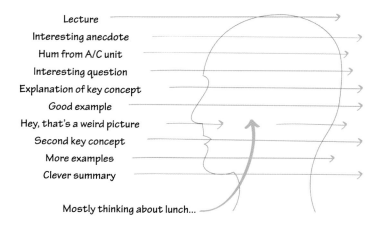

So, how do you get your learner's attention? Well, to do that, you have to talk to the elephant.

TALK TO THE ELEPHANT

Jonathan Haidt, in his book *The Happiness Hypothesis*, talks about the brain being like a rider and an elephant:

> *The rider is ... conscious, controlled thought. The elephant, in contrast, is every-thing else. The elephant includes the gut feelings, visceral reactions, emotions, and intuitions that comprise much of the automatic system.*

Basically, he is talking about the idea that there are two separate parts of your brain that are in control—the conscious verbal thinking brain and the automatic, emotional, visceral brain.

Haidt, 2006

THE RIDER

The rider part of your brain is the rational, Mr. Spock, control-your-impulses, plan-for-the-future brain. Your rider tells you all sorts of useful things that you know will provide long-term benefit.

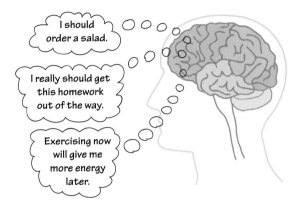

THE ELEPHANT

The elephant is your attracted-to-shiny-objects, what-the-hell, go-with-what-feels-right part of the brain. It's drawn to things that are novel, pleasurable, comfortable, or familiar.

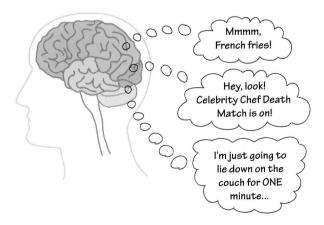

The elephant WANTS, but the rider restrains that wanting. This is a really useful evolutionary advantage—the rider allows you to plan ahead and to sacrifice short-term wants for long-term gains.

THE ELEPHANT IS BIGGER AND STRONGER

One of the challenges we all face, though, is that we have a tendency to overestimate the rider's control. The rider is our conscious verbal thinking, and because it talks to us, we tend to think it's in control.

And sometimes that thought seems justified, because (again, sometimes) the elephant is willing, and goes along with the rider pretty easily.

But other times, the elephant is going to do what it wants to, regardless of what the rider says.

And when the elephant and the rider are in serious conflict, guess who usually wins?

Exactly.

WHAT DOES THIS MEAN FOR YOUR LEARNERS?

Your learners have their own elephants:

They look uncomfortably familiar, don't they? The important point is, if the elephant isn't engaged, the learner is going to have a hell of a time paying attention. But the rider can *force* the elephant to pay attention. We do it all the time. Any time you have forced yourself to complete a complicated homework assignment, fill out a tax return, or understand a legal document, you've been dragging your elephant along.

There's a cost to this, though. Dragging an elephant where it doesn't want to go is exhausting, cognitively speaking. We have to expend a lot of willpower to make it happen, and willpower gets used up pretty quickly.

In a study (Shiv 1999) participants were asked to remember either a two-digit number or a seven-digit number. They were subsequently offered a snack choice of either fruit salad or a piece of cake.

or

Approximately twice as many people chose cake in the seven-digit group as in the two-digit group.

This suggests that the cognitive resources of memory, focus, and control are finite. You *can* control the elephant, just not for very long. There have been a number of studies that suggest that self-control is a limited and exhaustible resource (Gailliot 2007, Vohs 2007). If your learners are having to force themselves to pay attention, there's a limit to how long they are going to be able to exert the control necessary to do so.

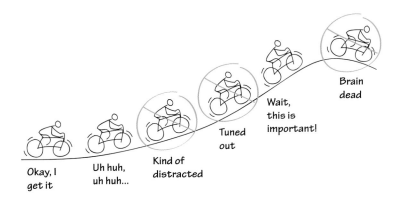

Asking your learners to rely entirely on willpower and concentration is like asking the rider to drag the elephant uphill. (Note: Bicycling images are based on work I did at Allen Interactions, and are used with their generous permission.)

Read the following paragraph:

> *Right-of-way and yielding laws help traffic flow smoothly and safely. They are based on courtesy and common sense. Violation of these laws is a leading cause of traffic crashes. When two vehicles reach an intersection at the same time, and there is no traffic light or signal, the driver of the vehicle on the left must yield to the vehicle on the right.*
>
> *When two vehicles reach an intersection at the same time, and all-way stop signs or flashing red traffic lights control the intersection, the driver on the left must yield right of way to the driver on the right. (Minnesota Driver's Manual, p. 41)*

How much effort did you have to put in to processing that text? It's not a particularly difficult concept, but your rider probably had to force your elephant to pay attention, and you had to put effort into translating the text into a visual so you could parse the information correctly.

Think about how that process *feels*. Unless you teach driver's ed or have a geeky fondness for driving regulations, it probably felt effortful and mildly unpleasant to have to force yourself to read and comprehend that passage. Just the kind of thing to make that chocolate cake look mighty appealing.

ATTRACT THE ELEPHANT

But if you can attract and engage the elephant, it means there's not nearly as much of a burden on the rider. Think about really great learning experiences you've had. They are probably ones that have engaged your interests and curiosity on a visceral or emotional level.

In the next section, we'll take a closer look at techniques for attracting the elephant, but all of them should be used with caution. The techniques that can be used effectively to attract the elephant can sometimes be *too* effective.

If the elements used to get the elephant's attention are not *intrinsic* to the learning subject matter and activities, then they can have a negative effect on learning and retention (Thalheimer 2004).

WAYS TO ENGAGE THE ELEPHANT

So, how do you attract and engage the elephant?

- Tell it stories
- Surprise it
- Show it shiny things
- Tell it all the other elephants are doing it
- Leverage the elephant's habits

TELL IT STORIES

Read the following story about a friend of mine:

> My friend Karen can't tell left from right. Just can't do it. When she really needs to know, she still holds up both hands to see which one forms the "L" for left.
>
> As you might imagine, this is a bit of a problem while she's driving. She has a hard time following directions, and meeting another car at a four-way stop is practically cause for a panic attack.
>
> She knows that the driver on the right gets to go first, but between the difficulty of figuring out which one is on the right, and the inevitable second-guessing of that, she ends up doing a dance of start-stop-staaaart-stop-STOP until she winds up waving the other driver through regardless of who actually had the right of way.
>
> I tried to convince her to put "Left" and "Right" signs in her car, but she said that was too embarrassing.
>
> In the end, we glued a small lighthouse statue (a relic of some childhood vacation to the seashore) to the far right side of her dashboard. We refer to it as her "Right-light," and she always tells herself that if the other car is on the right-light side, then that car has the right of way.

Compare the experience of reading that passage to the experience of reading the passage in the previous section. Which one required more effort? Was one passage easier to picture in your mind?

I think for most people, the story about Karen is probably easier to read, and easier to visualize. It's also likely that you could re-tell Karen's story with reasonable accuracy, even after some time has elapsed.

PEOPLE LIKE STORIES

We like stories. We learn a lot from stories, and we seem have a particularly good memory for them. A really well-told story can stick with us for years, even if we've only heard it once. In general, the elephant seems to be pretty willing to give stories an initial listen.

So what is it about stories that make them useful learning tools?

- **They go on existing shelves.** You already have a set of story shelves—you know how they work, and what the parts of a story are. You know there's usually a main character, some kind of problem, and then a resolution of that problem. Some of this is culturally derived. If you are from the USA you might have a different story template than someone from Japan or someone from Malawi, but you already have shelves on which to put the story details.
- **There's a logical flow.** Stories usually involve sequenced events, and frequently follow a chronological flow. You are more like to remember the sequence of crawl > walk > run than you are to remember the sequence of walk > run > crawl, because there's a logical flow. Part of the promise of stories is that they will also have a logical flow, and when you are recalling them, you can use that logic to recall what the events are. If someone retells the Karen story, they probably won't talk about the lighthouse on the dashboard before they talk about Karen's behavior at four-way stops.
- **Stories create suspense.** Whenever somebody starts telling you a story, there's an implied puzzle that you start trying to solve. What's the point of the story? Is it supposed to be funny? Is it going to be surprising? You start making predictions ("hmm...I know where this story is going...") or anticipating the purpose and outcome. The elephant likes puzzles (we'll talk more about this later in this chapter).
- **Stories aren't boring (we hope).** Of course there can be bad stories, or tedious stories (let's face it, the Karen story isn't going to win any literary awards), but when someone starts telling a story, the implied promise is that there's an interesting reason for this story and therefore you should pay attention.

THE HERO

Another way to leverage storytelling in learning design is to make people the heroes of their own story.

A friend of mine who is a game designer says the purpose of game design is to *make the player feel smart*. Sebastian Deterding, a game researcher and academic, describes it this way:

> *Games satisfy one of our three innate psychological needs—namely, the need to experience competence, our ability to control and affect our environment, and to get better at it. (Deterding 2011)*

I think we have a similar responsibility when we design learning experiences, but I think our responsibility is to make the learner feel *capable*.

So how can your learners feel more capable?

- **Show them the before and after.** Your learner should be able to see how they will be different if they master the skills. What will they be able to do that they can't do now? Will they be more capable? Will they be able to handle problems that they can't right now? Will they have new tools to put in their professional toolbox? Show the learners what they can do, and how they can get there.

Mild-mannered new hire

Help desk ninja

- **Give them real achievements.** Let them do meaningful things with the material while they are learning about it. Organize your content around those achievements. For example, which beginning Photoshop class would you rather take?

Photoshop for Beginners - Lesson Outline

Class A	Class B
Lesson 1: Working with layers	Lesson 1: How to create a swanky blog header
Lesson 2: Photo-editing tools	Lesson 2: How to make a so-so photo look amazing
Lesson 3: Working with filters and effects	Lesson 3: How to create an album cover
Lesson 4: Using the Pen tool	Lesson 4: How to remove your ex from your sister's wedding pictures

Which one is more likely to make the learner feel like they can actually accomplish something using the tool?

- **Create a first-person puzzle to solve.** Use a first-person story that runs through the whole learning experience. Say you're taking a sales course to teach you the features and benefits of a new product. How would you react to an opening slide that read "In this lesson, you will learn the features, benefits, and sales techniques for the Turboloader 3000" compared to one that showed a friendly agent in an open doorway, saying "The new Turboloader 3000 that just came in looks awesome! Hey, isn't your main client looking for a Turboloader? She's coming in today, isn't she?"

Suddenly, there's a *reason* to pay attention to the information. There's a goal, and time pressure, and a sense of urgency that "Learn about all the features and benefits of the Turboloader 3000" just doesn't instill.

URGENCY

Creating a sense of urgency is one of the biggest benefits you can get from using scenarios or stories in learning design.

Stephen Covey's 2x2 matrix of urgent vs. important tasks highlights the fact that we frequently attend to the urgent rather than the important. Of course, we deal first with things that are both urgent AND important, but after that, we tend to deal with the urgent (the email that just popped into the box) ahead of the important (the report due at the end of the week).

Important, but not urgent   Urgent, but not important

This is because the elephant is much more attuned to what feels urgent and immediate. While learning to focus on the important may be good life skill for individuals, it doesn't help you when designing learning that engages the elephant.

Remember the "things that can kill you" chart from Chapter 4? We are wired to pay attention to urgent things, because we evolved in an environment where "urgent" was frequently equivalent to "things that can kill you."

So which approach do you think would be more compelling for the elephant?

I wince now to think of when I was a new teacher, and said things like "This is really important stuff" or "You'll be really glad you know this stuff later on." You can't capture the elephant's attention by just *asserting* that a topic is important. The rider may believe you when you say things like that, but the elephant knows better.

So what elements can you use to create a sense of urgency?

- **A compelling story**—Use classic storytelling elements to create a compelling scenario. Have a protagonist who is trying to accomplish a goal. Have an antagonist who is preventing the protagonist from accomplishing that goal. Have obstacles along the way that the protagonist must overcome. Have an inciting incident that sets up the drama of the story—a conflict that needs to be resolved. Make it so the protagonist needs to change and grow to overcome the obstacles.
- **Showing, not telling**—The elephant is pretty smart. It's not just going to take your word for it that something is important. It wants to SEE and FEEL the importance. This is one of the golden rules of fiction writing and moviemaking: Avoid heavy-handed exposition, and use visuals, action, and dialogue instead.

- **Constraint of time or resources**—One indisputable way to raise the level of urgency is to create constraints. Give people time constraints or resource constraints and set them at a problem. Use caution here, however. Your learners will not appreciate having only five minutes to complete a 20-minute task. 15-18 minutes to complete a 20-minute task creates a sense of urgency. Five minutes to complete a 20-minute task creates pissed-off learners.

- **Immediacy**—In learning environments, we tend to focus on future consequences and outcomes, but the elephant is a creature of immediacy. Things that are going to happen in the future, regardless of how dire they are, are less compelling to the elephant than things that are happening RIGHT NOW. That's why "You may need to know these safety evacuation procedures" is far less compelling than "A fire just broke out on the 8th floor! Quick—what do you need to do first?"

- **Interesting dilemmas**—Give your learners interesting choices to make. Dilemmas capture attention if they are done well. The primary key to this is to not use right/wrong options. You can't wring much tension out of a right/wrong choice. Better options include choices between:

  - A good option and a very good option

  - Two bad options

  - Good, better, and best options

  - Two options that are each a mixture of good and bad, but in different ways.

  Well-designed games can provide fantastic examples of compelling dilemmas using constrained resources as pressure: Do you spend half your money to buy the railroad in Monopoly, knowing that it's a safer bet, but will ultimately be worth less than holding out for the third green property? Either choice could be good or bad depending on the circumstances.

- **Consequences, not feedback**—This goes back to the notion of show, don't tell, but use actual consequences rather than feedback when people make choices in a learning scenario.

EMOTIONAL RESONANCE

Stories have an emotional resonance that can help us form opinions and make decisions. You don't just want people to learn things—you want them to be able to act on what they learn, and emotional context helps them do that.

For a long time, there was a myth of "rational decision-making"—that the best way to make decisions was to rationally weigh the pros and cons, and not let messy emotions interfere.

Antonio Damasio, a behavioral neuroscientist, examined this idea by looking at patients who had brain damage in certain areas of the brain that support emotion. Rather than being clear and incisive decision-makers due to the absence of emotions, these patients found even simple decision-making to be extremely difficult. We seem to need an emotional "tug" to help us decide.

When we teach people facts, stripped of broader context, we make it hard for those learners to act on that information. Of course, the necessity of emotional context varies depending on the subject matter. If I'm creating learning materials to teach bar staff how to use a cash register, I'm not going to be overly concerned with the emotional context. If I'm teaching that same group how to ensure they aren't serving alcohol to underage or overly intoxicated drinkers, I'm going to be much more concerned about the emotional context.

Take a look at the following statement from a sales course:

The sales commission on repeat sales is 10%.

This looks like the mother of all objective facts, right? Just another certainty to put on your list. But what happens if we add a little emotional context to that fact?

Facts are frequently meaningless to us until we see them in some kind of broader context that allows us to begin to make judgments or sense about them.

Each of the pictures on the previous page tells us a different story about how we should feel about a 10% sales commission. Maybe it's an awesome thing because industry standard is 4%. Maybe it's infuriating because the salesperson is used to a 30% commission.

We believe that there are "objective facts," but all valuable information has meaning only in a bigger context, and part of that context is emotional. If you don't use that context in learning design, your learner may gather facts, but they won't know how to *feel* about those facts. If they don't know how to feel about them, they won't know what to do with them.

SURPRISE IT

One pretty sure-fire way to get the elephant's attention is to surprise it.

UNEXPECTED REWARDS

When researchers test people using expected and unexpected rewards, there is greater activation of anticipation and reward structures in the brain when the reward is unexpected (Berns 2001). Basically, people have a much stronger response to unexpected rewards than they do to ones they know are coming.

For example, when I was growing up, I got a birthday card from my grandmother every year with a check for five dollars. Now, this was always pleasing, because I love my grandmother and it was really sweet of her to do that, but the five dollars itself stopped being particularly exciting after about the age of twelve. There was always pleasure at the gesture from Grandma, but very little buzz around the money itself.

Compare that to the feeling you get when you are walking down the street and find five dollars lying on the ground, with no obvious owner in sight.

I don't know about you, but if I find five dollars lying on the ground, that's kind of awesome ("SCORE!"). And I probably keep a closer eye on the ground for a while after that happens.

The amount of money is the same in both examples, but the reaction is very different, due to the unexpectedness.

This tendency to react more strongly to unexpected rewards can be a valuable survival characteristic. Basically, if something is good, we want to remember that because we want MORE. And if something is bad, we want to remember that too, so we can avoid it in the future. But if something is *exactly the way we thought it would be*, there's really no reason to allocate mental resources to reinforcing that thought or idea.

Our apparently very-human reaction to an unexpected reward is a big part of why slot machines are so effective. They provide a variable reward schedule, which means we can't predict when we will get a win from the machine, so it's always a surprise when it happens. Unexpectedness is also part of our enjoyment of other entertainments, like sports or comedy.

Video games also do this well—we will be going along, collecting gold coins, when suddenly, after the 35th gold coin, we get the SUPER PLATINUM HAMMER OF DEATH. When something like that happens, we immediately start looking for the pattern. *What was I doing that caused that to happen? What can I do to make it happen again?*

In contrast, feedback in a lot of e-learning is almost mind-numbingly consistent:

> *Great job! You correctly identified Option A as the correct answer! That is correct!*
>
> Continue

There are reasons why consistency can be helpful. The main one is reducing *cognitive load*. If an interface element (like a feedback box) is consistent, then I learn it once and don't have to allocate mental resources toward identifying its purpose after that. The problem with too much consistency is that I will start to ignore the box altogether pretty quickly.

If you are in a training class for a new computer system, and the instructor says "OK, I'm going to start with the 37 main features of the system, with definitions of the functions for each feature," would you say "All right! Bring 'em on!" or would you say "Just kill me now..."?

But before you have a chance to say either, the instructor goes on to say "Just kidding—we're just going to focus on the three most critical features. The rest of that stuff is in your manuals." Would you be more likely to pay attention to those three features at that point?

DISSONANCE

Another form of surprise happens when we bump into something that doesn't match our view of the world. Basically, there's no place in our closet for it.

Let's say you are walking down the street one day, and you see a purple dog.

Now, we've already talked about how you probably have a whole set of shelves in your closet for dogs. You probably have a pretty detailed mental model for dogs. But unless you have a traumatic dog-painting incident in your childhood, you probably don't have "purple" as part of your mental dog-model.

So when you see the dog, you are comparing what you see with your existing formula for dogs (right size, right shape, right texture, right movement, right sounds—yep, it's a dog), but it's not the right color. There's enough there that *does* match your definition of dog, so you really don't question that, but you do stop at the color.

Now you have two opposing ideas in your head: "That's a purple dog" and "Dogs are not purple."

The term for this is *cognitive dissonance*—stuff just doesn't add up based on what you know about the world. You need to reconcile those two opposing viewpoints. How do you go about doing that? In the curious case of the dog, explanations could include:

- "Somebody spray-painted that poor dog."
- "I'm seeing things."
- "Maybe there really are purple dogs..."

In the last example, you are considering whether to reconcile and expand your mental model for dogs to include their being purple.

This is what some people will refer to as a "teachable moment." You get this nice element of friction that requires the learner to actively reconcile a disparate idea.

THE ELEPHANT IS A CURIOUS CREATURE

As my mother's first line of email tech support, I spend a lot of time on the AOL home page. AOL has a freakish ability to get me to follow article links, frequently for things that I don't care about at all:

- Which '80s child star now has three wives?
- 8 reasons to avoid lip balm
- The surprising truth about fluorescent lights

I really don't *care* about any of these things, yet find myself strangely compelled to click on them (I actually made up that list, but you get the idea). Whoever writes headlines for the AOL home page is a genius at tweaking my curiosity. It's shallow curiosity, but it still gets me to click on their link.

George Loewenstein, a professor of economics and psychology, describes curiosity as "arising when attention becomes focused on a gap in one's knowledge. Such information gaps produce the feeling of deprivation labeled *curiosity*. The curious individual is motivated to obtain the missing information to reduce or eliminate the feeling of deprivation."

The elephant is a curious creature, and if you can incite that curiosity, you can get a lot of attention from the elephant. So, how do you make the elephant curious?

- **Ask interesting questions**. If the question you are asking can be answered using a simple Google search, it's not an interesting question. Interesting questions require your learner to interpret or apply the information, not just to recall it. Pure recall questions were never all that interesting, but in today's current technology- and information-rich world, they are just a waste of time.

- **Be mysterious.** Can you set up a mystery that needs to be solved? Can you make use of clever reveals? Can you start a science class by asking "Why does Saturn have rings? And why don't any of the other planets in our solar system have them?" (Cialdini 2005) How about starting a project-management class with a case study where the project failed spectacularly, and challenging the students to spot the reasons from the initial project documents? You can use a mystery as a framing device for instruction, or as a puzzle for the students to solve.

- **Leave stuff out.** One of the ways the AOL headlines suck me in is by carefully leaving information out. It may turn out that the polygamist '80s child star is someone I barely remember from a show I never watched—or it might have been my absolute favorite actor from the show I watched religiously. The possibility is intriguing enough to pull me in. The reason I click is to close that knowledge gap.

  This is a tough idea for learning designers, because it's our job to make sure people have complete information, and easy access to it. Leaving key information out is counterintuitive.

- **Be less helpful.** Dan Meyer, a math teacher and blogger (http://blog.mrmeyer.com), has a philosophy he describes as Be Less Helpful. I encourage you to check out his material for yourself, but my understanding of what he talks about is that we do our learners a disservice by making the problem too complete. By putting less information into the upfront presentation of the problem, we encourage our learners to work to fill in the gaps and learn strategies for approaching messy, ill-structured problems, instead of just learning how to plug the numbers into a formula. Framing and clarifying the problem becomes part of the learning experience.

Ask Interesting Questions

Take a look at this passage from nineteenth-century educator and writer Charlotte Mason:

"Seeing that we are limited by the respect due to the personality of children we can allow ourselves but three educational instruments—the atmosphere of environment, the discipline of habit and the presentation of living ideas. Our motto is, 'Education is an atmosphere, a discipline, a life.' When we say that education is an atmosphere we do not mean that a child should be isolated in what may be called a 'child environment' specially adapted and prepared, but that we should take into account the educational value of his natural home atmosphere both as regards persons and things and should let him live freely among his proper conditions. It stultifies a child to bring down his world to the 'child's' level."

Let's say you are teaching this passage to an education class. You want to ask questions to engage the students. You could ask "What are the three educational instruments espoused by Charlotte Mason?" or "What does Charlotte Mason mean when she says "education is an atmosphere?"

You *could* ask those questions, but those questions suck. They are purely information-based questions, and can be answered by scraping content out of the passage. Instead, think about questions that require the learner to use and apply the content of the paragraph. For example:

- How could a modern educator "take into account the value of [a] natural home atmosphere"?
- Mason says it "stultifies a child to bring the world to the 'child's' level," but are there times when you have to do that?
- What do you think Mason would say about internet usage restrictions in schools?

Ask questions that require learners to create something new, or form an opinion, or apply a concept, not questions that require the rote recitation of information.

TELL IT ALL THE OTHER ELEPHANTS ARE DOING IT

The elephant is a social creature; one way to get the elephant's attention is to create a sense of social engagement. We pay more attention when there are other people involved.

In an experiment done by the MIT Media lab (Okita 2008), people interacted with a virtual agent in a virtual reality environment. In one group, the test subjects believed they were interacting with another person in avatar form; in the other, the test subjects knew they were interacting with a computer in humanoid form. In both cases, the test subjects were interacting with the computer, which behaved identically in both conditions.

When people believed they were interacting with a live person, they showed more visible signs of paying attention, learned more, and did better on post-tests. The only variable was that the test subjects believed they were interacting with a real person. Again, we pay more attention when there are other people involved.

Social learning can take many forms. It can involve group projects or be less formal knowledge exchanges using social media. In traditional learning environments, the teacher was the source of all knowledge—information was essentially handed to the students—but today, students bring a lot of knowledge and experience to any learning circumstance, and it's wasteful to not take advantage of that.

There are some specific ways to leverage social interaction to engage the elephant, including collaboration, competition, and social proof.

COLLABORATION

When you use collaborative learning, a number of social influences act to get the elephant involved. Group activities require negotiation, support, social obligations, and other small-group dynamics that require the elephant to engage and pay attention.

Collaborative learning has other benefits in addition to getting the elephant's attention. For example, Philip Uri Triesman, of the University of California – Berkeley, tells a story about trying to improve the math performance of minority students (primarily black and Hispanic students). Triesman and his colleagues speculated about possible causes of low performance—maybe the students hadn't had the same academic preparation at disadvantaged schools, or lacked good family support, or hadn't learned good study habits.

But when they investigated by actually observing the students, they found that none of these assumptions were true. They found that the minority students studied diligently and had supportive environments.

The clue came when Treisman and his colleagues compared the minority students' study habits to those of the much more academically successful Asian students. The main difference they found between the two populations was that the minority students studied alone, and the Asian students studied *together*.

The Asian students studied in groups, helped each other with problems, acted as resources for each other, and interacted socially around the subject matter. The minority students typically worked very hard, but worked alone, studying in isolation.

When Triesman and his colleagues created a structure to allow the minority students to work with each other, they became much more successful, equaling and frequently outperforming the rest of the students.

SOCIAL PROOF

Robert Cialdini, in his classic book *Influence: The Psychology of Persuasion*, talks about the principle of social proof—basically, the tendency of people to view an activity as more worthwhile if other people are doing it.

If learners can see that other learners are engaged with the material, or if a group of students know that previous classes performed well, they are more likely to engage and perform better themselves.

When I taught semester-long undergraduate classes, I would sometimes have students do class presentations throughout the semester. The tone and quality of the first few presentations would set the bar for the rest of the semester.

In an online learning environment, being able to see who else has taken a class or what their level of participation was can influence the behavior of subsequent students.

COMPETITION

Competition is a problem.

Competition is a social mechanism that equals instant urgency. Athletes who are about to compete start showing the physiological signs of arousal (increased heart rate, hormone release, skin reaction) before the physical part of the game even begins.

There's no question that competition can be a useful way to get the elephant's attention, but there are a number of problems with it as a learning strategy:

- **Not everyone is competitive.** Some people really enjoy competition, but some people really dislike it or find it stressful. While a little bit of tension can improve learning by focusing attention, a lot of stress will detract from the learning experience. Additionally, research suggests that it's a bigger negative for students who don't do well with competition than it is a positive for students who do respond well.
- **Competition teaches learners how to win.** Some people might say "what's wrong with teaching students how to win?" But a focus on winning can suck all the air out of the room. Basically, a focus on winning means learners are no longer focusing on the material. Winning becomes the main goal, not mastery of the material, or understanding, or how to use the material to accomplish things. All of those are relegated to the status of "things that will help me win" rather than being the goal itself.
- **Competition as motivation isn't a good long-term strategy.** It suggests to learners that things that aren't structured as a competition are less worthy of attention, and devalues the subject matter.

Competition can grab the elephant's attention, but should be used sparingly, if at all.

SHOW IT SHINY THINGS

There are a number of visual or tactile ways to attract the elephant's attention, including visual aids, humor, and rewards.

USE VISUALS, BUT BE CAREFUL

The elephant is very visual, and the images you use make a difference.

For example, we know (from earlier in this chapter) that this block of text isn't very engaging:

> *When two vehicles reach an intersection at the same time, and all-way stop signs or flashing red traffic lights control the intersection, the driver on the left must yield right of way to the driver on the right. (Minnesota Driver's Manual, p. 41)*

It does get better when we use a visual:

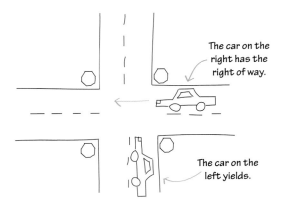

If you're looking for an even more dynamic example, think of car-racing video games. Video games are particularly masterful at creating visuals that attract (and possibly distract) the elephant.

There are several good resources on creating visuals. Robin William's *Non-Designer's Design Book* and Connie Malamed's *Visual Language for Designers* are particularly good. Those books can give you a lot of guidance around creating compelling visuals, but there are a few things you should keep in mind.

Know why you are adding a visual. Visuals can have a lot of different purposes in instructional material. It's useful to know why are you adding a graphic. Some of the reasons to use visuals include:

- Decoration—Sometimes it's just about making it pretty. Breaking up text or adding visual appeal both have their place. Don Norman's book *Emotional Design* discusses research suggesting that attractive things work better than unattractive ones—possibly due to the positive reaction they bring out in users—and it can be useful to provide visual rests in lengthy text passages. Despite that, decorative graphics are the shallowest type of instructional visual, and should be used with some caution. There is research that suggests decorative graphics can distract learners from the main material (Thalheimer 2004).

  Also, whenever possible, avoid visual clichés. We've all seen that generic "hand-shaking" stock art image too many times already.

- Progression—Sometimes visuals can be much more effective than a text-only explanation for showing a process or steps in a procedure. Visuals can be particularly useful in showing progression over time.

- Conceptual metaphorical—Visuals can help explain concept or a metaphor in a way that description alone can't. Infographics are specifically intended to make complicated information easier to process or understand.

Without a background in mathematics, data analysis, or similar fields that require spending lots of time with big numbers, most people have a hard time comprehending unfamiliar numeric-based data in any meaningful way. Visualization can help people understand how to process that information when they don't already have a set of shelves in their mental model.

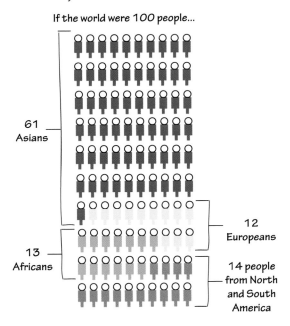

If the world were 100 people...

Visuals help distribute the load. Verbal and visual information seem to be processed differently by the brain, and as a result, effective use of both visual and verbal information help keep learners from being overwhelmed by the material, and give them more ways to find the information again.

Anyone who's read a typical textbook knows it's got a *lot* more verbal information than visual information. To use our shelf metaphor, there's a whole lot of capacity on the visual side of the shelf that isn't being used. As I mentioned in Chapter 1, learning styles (e.g., visual, auditory, kinesthetic learners) aren't very useful, and part of the reason is that *everyone is a visual learner.* Unless someone has a vision or related impairment, they learn from visuals, and if we aren't taking advantage of that capacity, we are tying one hand behind our backs as learning designers.

Visuals can help build shelves. If your learners have pretty small, general closets, and you have a lot of information to give them to put in those closets, visuals can be a good way to help them build a few shelves. Visual organizers can give learners a way to mentally parse the information they are receiving.

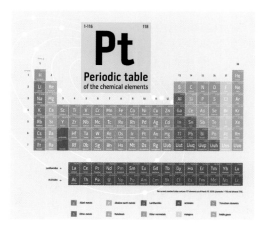

Visuals provide context. We've already talked about the critical importance of context, and visuals can provide a huge amount of context in a situation:

- Scenario context—You can spend a lot of time describing a scenario in words, or you can shortcut a lot of that wordiness using visuals. The setting where something takes place can provide a lot of information or triggers about a situation.

- Emotional context—Similarly, you can get a lot of emotional context from images. How much can you infer about each image below without having any words of explanation?

- Contextual triggers—One of the things we can do in a learning environment is to accustom our learners to certain behavior triggers.

  For example, I've recently been involved with a project where we want to educate people about "vampire" energy use—energy drawn from items like electronic devices that are plugged but not currently being used. If you leave a cell phone charging overnight, the charger continues to draw power after the phone is fully charged, wasting energy. We want the learner to associate the sight of a cell phone plugged in with the idea of potential wasted energy and then, consequently, with the action of unplugging fully charged phones.

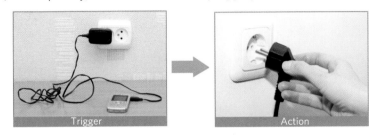

  Creating the visual association between the trigger and the action is an important part of encouraging the memory and the behavior.

LET THE ELEPHANT PLAY WITH STUFF

The elephant is also a tactile creature. When the elephant is difficult to corral, you can use hands-on methods to create engagement. You can use auditory, visual, and physical stimulation to attract attention.

Things that you can taste, touch, hear, and smell provide additional context that can act as memory triggers, and physical interaction can attract the elephant's attention by providing a different way to interact with material.

If what you are teaching has a hands-on component, then the learning should, too.

MAKE WITH THE FUNNY

Let's just get this out of the way first: HUMOR IS SUBJECTIVE. Not everyone finds the same things funny. That makes using humor for learning a somewhat tricky business.

That said, if you are confident of your audience, and confident that something is actually funny, then it can be used to good effect in engaging learners. Research studies have showed that students were better able to recall and complete funny sentences as opposed to neutral sentences, probably because the humor focuses learners' attention or because the humorous versions were more memorable (Schmidt 1994).

If you are trying to use humor, it's a really really good idea to test it with your audience to make sure they agree with you about what's funny.

Some people think there's nothing funnier than a disgruntled kitten in a frog costume.

And some people really don't.

PRIZES! REWARDS! STUFF!

Another way to attract the elephant's attention is to let it know that there are prizes or rewards.

But good use of rewards, like humor, can be a tricky business. At the most basic level, the idea is that if you reward a behavior, you increase the likelihood that behavior will occur, and if you punish a behavior, you decrease the likelihood that behavior will occur.

This can work if it's applied well in the right circumstances, but frequently, it's not applied well.

WHAT'S GOOD ABOUT REWARDS

The best thing about these kinds of rewards is that they provide a certain immediacy, which helps keep the elephant engaged.

Let's say I want to learn financial literacy and investing for retirement, so I get a book on the topic. It tells me all sorts of useful things, but some of them I will have to wait until next quarter to implement (changing a payroll deductions), and some I won't be able to use potentially for years (how to best distribute my IRA income after retirement). But there isn't anything I can *do* with most of this information *right now*, which, as you might imagine, makes it a bit difficult to force myself to pay attention to it.

Compare that to learning about financial investing using a simulation game. You sit down, create an avatar and start setting up your financial investment portfolio. You get to make decisions and play them through, skipping ahead years and decades at a time. You tweak and adjust your financial plan, and see how those decisions play out. You get to try completely different scenarios and see completely different outcomes.

The game scenario has a number of shiny advantages for attracting the elephant (feedback, risk, context, interesting and even fun challenges), but it also has the immediate rewards, punishments, and consequences that make it a compelling and "graspable" learning experience.

Don't get me wrong; books can have rewards too—it's not just the media that makes a difference. For an information junkie, the confirmations of already-gained knowledge and the new insights gained in books might provide a satisfying reward, but if you're not intrinsically motivated by the topic, you might need more specific challenges to accomplish, and more concrete rewards, in order to succeed in learning.

In the simulation example, there's something you can *do* immediately with the information you are learning. You don't have to work nearly as hard to persuade the elephant to pay attention, because the problem and questions are immediate.

WHAT'S BAD ABOUT REWARDS

But external rewards are a mixed bag. We've seen how they can be effective, but they can easily be mis-used. A good reward can be a moment of insight, a successful retirement portfolio in a simulation, or solving a puzzle. A bad reward is something that is extrinsic to the experience.

Here's the main thing you need to know:

Extrinisic rewards can demotivate people.

You could hand out extrinsic rewards like candy ("Finish this course and get a gift card!"), but that's a shallow and ultimately ineffective way to motivate someone. It might work with pets, but it's a bad method for people. I've started referring to this as "the gift card effect." You know the drill—"We can't actually compensate you appropriately for this, but if you do it anyway, you can enjoy the equivalent of three pricey Coffee Beverages on us instead!" As a gesture of appreciation after the fact, these cards are fine. As a way to incent or motivate behavior, they are at best silly, and at worst counter-productive.

Dan Ariely, a behavioral economist, did an experiment in which people were paid to make LEGO® shapes—a small sum for each shape they created. In one group, each LEGO shape was displayed prominently when it was completed, and in the other each shape was broken back apart in front of the person, and the pieces dumped back in the bins to be re-used (Ariely 2008).

Participants in the first group made significantly more shapes than people in the second, even though the financial rewards were exactly the same.

Similar effects are seen where people are asked to engage in an activity for the sake of that activity, rather than for financial payment or other extrinsic reward. Once you start paying people, it becomes work, and can have a negative effect on performance and motivation. For example, kids who are rewarded for drawing pictures draw *less* than when it is a voluntary activity. It becomes work, or an obligation, when there's compensation involved. The emphasis can very quickly shift from the activity to the rewards (Kohn 1993).

Two excellent books on this topic are *Drive* by Daniel Pink and *Punished by Rewards* by Alfie Kohn.

MAKING REWARDS MORE INTRINSIC

Rewards can be great motivators if they are intrinsic. Intrinsic rewards can take many forms, including (but not limited to) the satisfaction provided by the activity itself, the pleasure in a new capability, and the anticipation of being able to use new skills.

The common thread of all successful intrinsic rewards is that they need to be genuinely useful or satisfying to the learner. For example, we already talked about organizing a learning experience around real achievements:

Photoshop for Beginners
Lesson 1: How to create a swanky blog header
Lesson 2: How to make a so-so photo look amazing
Lesson 3: How to create an album cover
Lesson 4: How to remove your ex from your sister's wedding pictures

This learning experience has intrinsic rewards built right in, in the form of quantifiable and satisfying accomplishments. You can also consider how you would reward the different accomplishments. For example, you could give a big gold star and 1,000 experience points to learners for each item they accomplish, but that's a pretty extrinsic type of reward.

A better reward might be to create an online gallery where learners could display the results of their accomplishments. This form of reward would be much closer to the intrinsic nature of the task.

YOU DON'T GET TO DECIDE

There's one catch to designing for intrinsic rewards:

You don't get to decide what's intrinsic to the learner.

Basically, any form of intrinsic reward has to be flexible and has to ensure the learner has at least some control. If there aren't options and autonomy for the learners, then you are just guessing what is meaningful to them. Sometimes you may guess right (and the likelihood of that goes up when you really know your learner well), but ultimately you want to give the learner as much control as possible in letting them decide what's meaningful.

I've heard the argument that learners don't know what they don't know, and that they need guidance and directions. This can be a justification for less autonomy in an environment, but there are always ways to give options to even the most novice learners.

Some ways you can give learners autonomy:

- Let them help determine what's learned.
- Let them choose where to start, or what order to approach the material.
- Have them make decisions about what assignments or projects they do.
- Have them bring their own questions, projects, or problems to the table, and focus the learning experience around addressing or solving those challenges.

If you genuinely can't give learners any autonomy, then stay away from any kind of rewards as a way to drive attention.

 ## SUMMARY

- If you want to get and maintain your learners' attention, you need to talk to the emotional, visceral brain (elephant) as well as the conscious, verbal brain (rider).

- *Attracting* attention is not the same thing as *maintaining* attention. Make sure the device you use to attract attention is intrinsic to the material being learned. If it's not, it may actually be distracting, and negatively impact learning.

- Some ways to attract your learners' attention include stories, emotional resonance, urgency, surprise, and interesting puzzles.

- Social interaction and visual cues will go a long way to attracting and maintaining attention.

- Devices like competition and extrinsic rewards will attract your learners' attention, but they will almost certainly distract them from the real goal and have a negative impact on their intrinsic motivation. They are best avoided unless used very carefully.

- Intrinsic rewards almost always require learner autonomy or choice to be effective.

REFERENCES

Ariely, Dan, Emir Kamenica, and Drazen Prelec. 2008. Man's search for meaning: The case of Legos. *Journal of Economic Behavior & Organization* 67: 671–677.

Bean, Cammy. 2011. Avoiding The Trap Of Clicky-Clicky Bling-Bling. *eLearn Magazine,* June. http://elearnmag.acm.org/featured.cfm?aid=1999745

Berns, Gregory S., Samuel M. Mcclure, and P. Read Montague. 2001. Predictability modulates human brain response to reward. *Journal of Neuroscience* 21 (April).

Cialdini, Robert. 2005. What's the best secret device for engaging student interest? The answer is in the title. *Journal of Social and Clinical Psychology* 24 (1): 22–29.

Deterding, Sebastian. 2011. A Quick Buck by Copy and Paste, posted by *Gamification Research Network.* http://gamification-research. org/2011/09/a-quick-buck-by-copy-and-paste

Gailliot, M.T., R.F. Baumeister, C.N. DeWall, J.K. Maner, E.A. Plant, D.M. Tice, L.E. Brewer, and B.J. Schmeichel. 2007. Self-control relies on glucose as a limited energy source: Willpower is more than a metaphor. *Journal of Personality and Social Psychology* 92: 325–336.

Haidt, Jonathan. 2006. *The Happiness Hypothesis: Finding Modern Truth in Ancient Wisdom.* New York: Basic Books.

Jabr, Ferris. 2010. The Psychology of Competition: Meeting Your Match. *Scientific American Mind* Nov/Dec: 42–45.

Kohn, Alfie. 1993. *Punished by Rewards: The Trouble with Gold Stars, Incentive Plans, A's, Praise, and Other Bribes.* Boston: Houghton Mifflin.

Loewenstein, G. 1994. The Psychology of Curiosity: A Review and Reinterpretation. *Psychological Bulletin* 116 (1): 75–98. Found via Stephen Anderson's excellent article in Johnny Holland.

Mason, Charlotte. 1923. Three Instruments of Education, *Charlotte Mason's Original Homeschooling Series* 6: 94. Copyrighted 2002-2003 by Ambleside Online.

"Minnesota Driver's Manual." http://www.dps.state.mn.us/dvs/DLTraining/ DLManual/DLManual.htm

Okita, S.Y., J. Bailenson, and D.L. Schwartz. 2008. Mere Belief of Social Action Improves Complex Learning. *Proceedings of the 8th International Conference for the Learning Sciences.*

Pink, Daniel. 2009. *Drive: The Surprising Truth About What Motivates Us.* New York: Riverside (Penguin).

Shiv, B. and A. Fedorikhin. 1999. Heart and Mind in Conflict: Interplay of Affect and Cognition in Consumer Decision Making. *Journal of Consumer Research* 26 (December): 278–282.

Thalheimer, W. 2004 (November). Bells, whistles, neon, and purple prose: When interesting words, sounds, and visuals hurt learning and performance—a review of the seductive-augmentation research. http://www.work-learning.com/seductive_ augmentations.htm

Treisman, Philip Uri. 1990. Academic Perestroika: Teaching, Learning, and the Faculty's Role in Turbulent Times. From an edited transcript of his lecture of the same name, delivered March 8, 1990, at California State University, San Bernardino. http://www2.ed.gov/about/offices/list/ope/fipse/ perestroika.html

Vohs, Kathleen D. and R. J. Faber. 2007. Spent Resources: Self-Regulatory Resource Availability Affects Impulse Buying. *Journal of Consumer Research* (March 2007).

DESIGN FOR KNOWLEDGE

(In which we learn to not hand out
mittens in summertime, and
to let learners hold the map)

SOME OF THE CHALLENGES

I've struggled a bit with what to include in this chapter. On one hand, designing for knowledge is probably a whole book unto itself; on the other hand, pretty much everything we've already talked about is part of designing for knowledge.

So in this chapter, we're going to focus on a few basic questions:

- Will your learners remember?
- Does the learner understand?
- How much guidance do you give learners?

We'll also take a look at a process for designing learning solutions.

WILL THEY REMEMBER?

Let's look at a few of the many ways to make content more memorable.

MAKE SURE THE CLOSET, ER, GROUND, IS FERTILE

One way to embed content more firmly in memory is to already have some shelves the learner can use to store the information.

HAVE LEARNERS CONSIDER WHAT THEY ALREADY KNOW

A lot of times learners already have some knowledge of a topic, and you can draw that out. For example, if you are teaching a group of people how to write good job descriptions, you can ask the group to tell you everything they think needs to go into a job description, and then work from that list.

Collecting such a list from learners accomplishes two key things. It gets them to dust off and look at their existing shelves for job descriptions, and it has them think actively about what the shelves should be for writing job descriptions.

POSITION TITLE
What I know about job descriptions

KEY RESPONSIBILITIES
What I know about job descriptions

QUALIFICATIONS
What I know about job descriptions

After you've generated the list, you can edit it, adding missing elements or removing some items as you go. If you need to remove something, that becomes an active process ("Here's why this isn't necessary...").

Instead of trying to just remember what you said, learners are actively stimulating and adapting their existing model.

Whenever you want to tell your learners something, first ask yourself if there's any way they can tell *you*, instead.

HAVE LEARNERS CONSTRUCT THEIR OWN FRAMEWORK OF SHELVES

Metacognition is a term that loosely means "thinking about thinking." Among other things, it means being aware of how you are learning.

Hmm, what do I know?

What do I not know?

What am I not sure of?

You can have students take an active role in their own metacognition. For example, problem-based learning is a teaching method originally developed in medical schools, to supplement or replace pure information-delivery teaching methods.

Traditionally, medical students, being a motivated bunch, learned information really well, but couldn't always apply it. Problem-based learning was intended to help them better apply the information they'd learned.

An example of problem-based learning might work roughly like this: A facilitator gives a small group of students a case ("A 38-year old female with chest pains and dizziness"), and the students proceed to diagnose the patient. While the students are working through the case, they keep track of a few categories on a whiteboard.

Facts	Ideas	Learning Issues
What do we know?	What are our hypotheses?	What are our knowledge gaps?

The whiteboard is a way the students can keep an explicit list of what they know, what they think, and where they don't know enough. Frequently, students are given the responsbility of investigating the areas on the learning issues list and bringing the information back to the group. This can vary depending on how a particular problem-based learning lesson is designed, but one of the fundamental ideas is to make the students aware of their own knowledge, and, even more importantly, of the *gaps* in their knowledge.

Another way to have your learner be more aware of their own learning, is to give learners an inventory of the content, and have them rate their level of comfort with each topic. As they go, they can adjust their ratings, either as they get more comfortable, or as they realize they don't know as much as they thought they did. While these ratings don't mean the learners have actual proficiency, it does involve them in tracking their own understanding, and focuses them on eliminating gaps.

MAKE IT STICKY

Imagine you work taking the ticket stubs in a movie theater. You rip tickets for hundreds of people every day. At the end of the day, how many of those people do you think you remember?

You are only going to remember the people who really stood out, right? This isn't a failing of your memory—it's how things are supposed to work. If something isn't signficant, important, or unusual, why would we want to remember it?

The problem occurs when we can't hold onto things that we *want* to remember.

In Chapter 4, we talked about how working memory has a really short duration, and you forget most of the things you have in working memory unless you are actively trying to keep them there through rehearsal, or because they are significant or memorable.

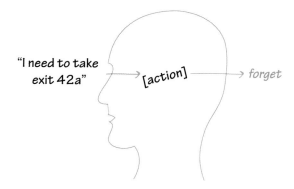

If something doesn't stand out for some reason, there's a good chance it will just pass through without leaving much of a mark, like water through a pipe.

This can be particularly true if it is information the learner already thinks they know or understand—why would you pay attention to something you already know?

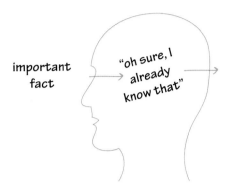

We seem to be particularly susceptible to this one—the one where we already think we know the material—which is problematic for two reasons. First, it may be a problem because we may not know it *enough*. In Chapter 4, we looked at how it's more difficult to *recall* something as opposed to just *recognizing* it. We may think we can recall, when all we can do is recognize. The second possible reason that this is a problem is because we may only *think* we understand; we may actually have misconceptions or incomplete understandings that we don't realize we have.

In a research study (Muller 2008) that looked at using videos to teach science concepts, students who received only clear, well-explained, visual explanations of physics concepts rated the videos highly, saying that they were indeed clear and easy to understand.

Another group of students were first shown videos that had explanations or dialogues between two characters discussing common misconceptions about physics principles, and then they (the students, not the characters) were given the explanation of those principles.

The group that heard the discussions of the misconceptions rated the videos *less* easy to understand—they were more confused than if they had received only the explanation. The second group also did much better on the post-test, and showed significantly more improvement over the first group.

So, even though the second group felt *more confused*, they actually understood much better. Arguably, this has to do with them having their assumptions confronted, and having to actively reconcile misconceptions.

CREATING FRICTION

Learning is messy, and interacting with and resolving that messiness can help embed the information into long-term memory. We want learners to engage with the material.

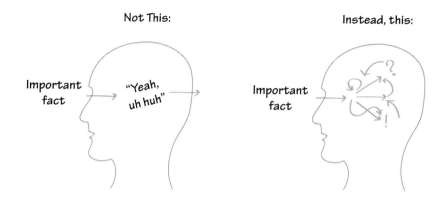

Passive experiences like lectures or page-turner e-learning courses, where the information is just channeled to the learner, can also flow smoothly right *by* the learner. If the learner is actively engaging with or interested in the material, then a passive information-delivery system can still be an effective tool. But if your learner is even mildly disengaged, this same method probably won't accomplish much. Creating opportunities to interact with the material can make a lesson even more engaging for your motivated learners.

If you don't want the material to flow smoothly past (or around) your learners, then you want to provide a little friction—something that requires learners to chew on the material, cognitively speaking.

We've already talked about a number of ways to make the learning experience more interactive, which is the main way you can add friction, but let's take a look at a few more.

SHOW, DON'T TELL

Cathy Moore, an outstanding e-learning designer (http://www.cathy-moore.com), has a checklist of items that she uses to evaluate whether or not a learning experience is action-oriented, or more of an info dump. One of the criteria she looks at is whether the course **shows** or **tells**:

> *...feedback that **shows** learners what happens as a result of their choice; learners draw conclusions from the result.*

> *vs.*

> *...feedback that explicitly **tells** learners "correct" or "incorrect;" learners aren't allowed to draw conclusions.*

> *(Moore 2011)*

One of the reasons this is important is that *telling* is smooth, but *showing* has friction: it requires learners to make some of their own connections to interpret what's going on.

Showing rather than telling is a big theme in fiction writing:

> *The difference is that in telling there's absolutely no role for the viewer or the reader to put anything together. In showing, the viewer has a chance... to put stuff together themselves and to be active in the story.*

> *It's so much more engaging as an audience member if I am left to put stuff together myself and not have it all assembled for me and handed to me...*

> *You need to give your readers stuff to do. Give them a way to be an active participant, and by allowing them to draw conclusions based on little clues that you leave, you engage them in the story and they become part of it.*

> *—Lani Diane Rich, Storywonk Daily*

Arguably, reading fiction is not interactive in the same way as a classroom activity or an e-learning simulation, but even how something is written can allow the learner a more or a less active role.

There's other research that bears this out. In one study (Kuperberg 2006), subjects were shown sentence pairs. Some of the sentence pairs went together very easily (x obviously causes y), some required some interpretation to see the connection, and some were pretty unrelated. One of the (somewhat violent) examples from the study is:

Main sentence: *"The next day his body was covered in bruises."*

That sentence was preceded by one of these statements:

"Joey's brother punched him again and again." (highly causally related— x obviously caused y)

"Joey's brother became furiously angry with him." (intermediately causally related—you've got to read between the lines a little)

"Joey went to a neighbor's house to play." (pretty much unrelated)

The subjects spent the most time on the middle sentences—they were related but forced the subjects to connect some dots to see the connection. The study saw a greater degree of brain activation in many areas for those sentences, and they were better remembered later.

So, if people have to make the connections themselves, it's likely they'll remember more later.

Ways to show, rather than tell

Tell	Show
"In this lecture, we'll discuss the five primary ways that criminals can use the stock exchange to launder money…"	"You are an embezzler, and you need to hide $800,000 in illicit funds. What's the first thing you can do to launder the money? Choose one of the options below…"
"You chose to offer the customer the XYZ model of refrigerator, but that model is too expensive for this customer. The ABC model would have been a better choice."	"The customer shrugs and says 'I'll think about it' before he wanders off in the direction of the dishwashers. Try the scenario again, and see if you can be more successful with a different model."
Driver's Ed teacher: "Here are the rules for when you encounter a school bus. First, if the light is flashing…"	Driver's Ed teacher: "So, what do you think are the biggest concerns with a stopped school bus? What would people be worried about?…Right—they'd be worried about kids exiting and crossing the street…"
"A highly irate woman comes into the restaurant…"	A 50-ish woman in a business suit slams into the restaurant and charges up to you. "Look!" she says "I come in here ALL THE TIME, and I am not used to being treated like this…"
"One of the biggest issues with project management is scope creep. Let's list some ways that scope creep can happen…"	"OK, class, you all had update meetings with your project clients this week. What issues came up? Were there any problems with the deliverables you had due this week?"

For the following three scenarios, how could you change them from tell to show? Consider each scenario again before reading the design solution below (which is of course just one of many possible solutions).

Scenario 1: "Here's an example of a balanced 2,000 calorie a day diet. It's been carefully balanced to contain 55% carbohydrates, 15% protein, and 30% fat."

Solution 1: "You need to create a balanced 2,000 calorie diet that is approximately 55% carbohydrates, 15% protein, and 30% fat. Choose foods from each of the categories to create your meal plan for the day. Make sure you also select a quantity. When you're done, I'll give the nutritional information for the food lists, and you can see how close you came, and what you would need to adjust to meet the requirements."

Scenario 2: "When determining employee compensation levels, you want to take years of experience, qualifications, and the pay rate of comparable employees into consideration."

Solution 2: "Take a look at Jane's qualifications and company history. She's being promoted into your department. How much are you going to pay her? Here's the same information for the other four members of your department, plus the salary histories for each employee."

Scenario 3: "The red highlight shows you where to click to open the customer record. Click the highlighted area, and then click next to move to the next screen."

Solution 3: "Where do you think you would need to click on this screen to open the customer record? If you get stuck, you can consult the Help function, or you can request a hint."

SOCIAL FRICTION

Another way to add some friction to learning is to use interpersonal interaction. Each learner is going to bring their own perspectives and experience to the table, and sharing and debating can be good ways to engage with a topic.

Discussion topics can facilitate this ("discuss the consequences of sexual harassment complaints in the broader organization"), but you generally get better results if you give groups a more concrete purpose. They could:

- Create something
- Work together to teach something to the rest of the class
- Argue different sides of a debate
- Investigate and report back (e.g., find three good examples, or a bad example, and bring them back to the class)

Let's say you are teaching a group how to write a good help-wanted advertisement. You could employ small group interaction by having the learners:

- Work together to create a job advertisement for a position
- Research different aspects of equal employment guidelines and present that information back to the class
- Rank-order five advertisements you've given them, from best to worst, and why
- Identify all the problems with some bad job listings you provide
- Research online and find three good job listings to bring to the class, with the criteria they used

Requiring all of these activities would clearly be overkill (and of course these suggestions are not exhaustive), but social interaction can be a good source of learning friction, so you want a variety of ways to include and leverage that.

HELPING YOUR LEARNERS UNDERSTAND

You don't just want your learners to remember—you also want them to *understand.*

The first part of helping ensure that your learners will understand what you want to teach them is to start with the right content.

The right content is:

- Less than you think it is
- Enough detail but no more
- Relevant to the learners
- Stuff that can fit in their closet, with some expansion or rearranging

THE RIGHT AMOUNT OF CONTENT

What's the right amount of content for your learners? Probably less than you think it should be. Working memory has a pretty limited capacity (we talked about this in Chapter 4), and it's highly likely that you'll want to communicate more content than your learners are in a position to take in.

It might help to think about it this way:

You can keep handing material to your learners, but you can't make them carry it around. Look closely at the material you want to communicate, and focus on the parts that are most relevant to learners. Anything else, you may need to provide as a resource for them later. Be ruthless about including only what's really necessary.

For example, let's say you want to teach somebody who has never baked how to make an apple pie. When it comes time to give instructions about putting on the top crust, don't digress into alternate explanations of how you can also do a lattice top, or a streusel, or a side discussion about different theories of steam vents, or a lengthy explanation about the way the proteins react if you overwork the gluten in the dough.

If someone is new to baking, stick with one way to do things. You can always elaborate later.

It's really easy to overestimate the right level of detail for your audience. The best way to know how much is too much is to try it out, and see how they do.

The important part of trying it out is to *start lean*, and test your content with your audiences to see where the holes are. Start with as little as you can get away with. If it's not enough, you'll find out quickly, because the learner will be confused, or will have questions. The gaps will bubble up like leaks in a submerged air mattress. If you start with too much, it'll be harder to identify those excesses. You might be able to tell where you are really overloading your learners, but a lot of the little extras might not be immediately visible as extraneous.

The Average Attention Span

Every once in a while I see some statement about learners' average attention spans. Maybe you've seen proclamations that "the average adult attention span is no more than 10 minutes" or 15 minutes, or 45 minutes, or...

If you think about it, this is just silly.

There's a movie theater near my house that shows a back-to-back marathon of all the *Lord of the Rings* movies every holiday season, and it's really well attended. And it's the *extended* editions of each movie.

That's over ELEVEN HOURS of movies, people. That's the attention span of that audience—*over eleven hours*.

Aside from the constraints of hunger, fatigue, and bathroom breaks, there's really no limit on someone's potential attention span. What may be much more limited is the length of time someone can *force themselves* to pay attention. Remember the elephant? If the elephant is happily romping with the hobbits, then attention is easy, but if you are asking your learners to corral the elephant, then the clock is probably ticking. You might be lucky to get 10 minutes from someone if you are explaining the procedures for their health savings account.

It's still not really plausible to put a number on it, though. It depends on too many variables—how much sleep that person got, whether they ate breakfast, if they are interested or motivated about the topic, whether the presentation is dynamic or monotone. There's really no way to say.

We've already talked about *getting* learners' attention, but there are also things you can do as a learning designer to *keep* learners interested:

- Be entertaining. This works, but can frequently be the most difficult to pull off (particularly you aren't naturally the life of the party). Still, there's a lot to be learned from entertainment media (movies, TV, games, etc.) about being more entertaining. There are also some good resources on being more engaging. Some recommendations include *Made to Stick* by Chip and Dan Heath, *Resonate* by Nancy Duarte, and *Presentation Zen* by Garr Reynolds.
- Ask questions. It's a lot harder to disengage if you have to think about how to respond.
- Change it up. Mix together presentation and activities and types of media.
- Have them interact. It's a lot of pressure on you to provide all the interaction; let learners interact with each other.
- Have them make stuff. Don't just have activities, have activities where they make stuff.

MISCONCEPTIONS

Another issue you'll have to contend with is learners' misconceptions. There are a couple of strategies that can help prevent misconceptions.

First, as we've looked at in previous chapters, you want to make sure you know what your learners are getting. Having good feedback loops, where you get learners to answer questions, give examples, and explain an idea or concept back to you, are all ways to do this.

Another strategy is using *examples* and *counter-examples*. If you ever read *Highlights* magazine in your dentist's waiting room as a child, you might remember the two characters Goofus and Gallant. Goofus always got it wrong, while Gallant always got it right. Goofus would take the last piece of fruit for himself, while Gallant would generously share his orange. The Goofus and Gallant comics were classic examples of the matching an example with a non- or counter-example.

This technique can be particularly effective in preventing misconceptions. For example, when I learned about writing survey questions in graduate school, the professor had us look at terrible survey questions to learn how to write good ones.

Let's say you want to teach someone about writing good true/false questions. You could explain some of the guidelines:

Guidelines for Good True/False Questions
Ask about only one thing at a time.
Test for knowledge, not memorization.
Avoid using qualifying words.

That's OK, but you'd probably want to elaborate with some examples:

Guidelines for Good True/False Questions	Example
Ask about only one thing at a time.	The guideline for the minimum following distance while driving is the 4-second rule. (True / False)
Test for knowledge, not memorization.	A 130-lb woman can consume 3 12-oz beers in an hour and feel confident she has a blood alcohol content within legal guidelines for driving. (True / False)
Avoid using qualifying words.	When you hear an emergency siren while driving, you should pull over. (True / False)

OK, so the examples *help*, but what if we add counter-examples?

Guidelines for Good True/False Questions	Good Example	Bad Example
Ask about only one thing at a time.	The guideline for the minimum following distance while driving is the 4-second rule. (True / False)	Safe following distance while driving can be measured using the 4-second rule or by having two car lengths between you and the other vehicle. (True / False)
Test for knowledge, not memorization.	A 130-lb woman can consume 3 12-oz beers in an hour and feel confident she has a blood alcohol content within legal guidelines for driving. (True / False)	The formula for determining blood alcohol content is %BAC = (A x 5.14/W x r) - .015 x H. (True / False)
Avoid using qualifying words.	When you hear an emergency siren while driving, you should pull over. (True / False)	When you hear an emergency siren while driving, you should always pull over immediately. (True / False)

How much do the counter-examples help clarify the concept being described? In this instance, you could use five good examples of how to write a particular survey questions, and not clarify the concept as much as you would by matching one good example with a single counter-example.

Another really useful way to use counter-examples is to use them to present the information in the first place, rather than starting with the concepts.

For example, if you wanted to teach learners how to write a good job description, you could give them a few terrible job descriptions, and then have them identify all the issues. Then you could use that learner-generated list to create the "good" guidelines.

HOW MUCH GUIDANCE?

I'm always anxious when I give people directions. I worry that I won't be clear enough, and the people will wind up hopelessly lost, wandering in circles and cursing my very bad-directions-giving existence.

Creating a learning experience involves giving directions, ideally ones that won't leave your learner wandering aimlessly.

So, how do you prefer to give directions?

I give step-by-step instructions–the person just needs to follow them exactly, and they'll be fine.

I like to sketch out a map that shows all the big streets, and then draw their specific route to it.

I don't really like to give directions unless I can put the actual map in front of a person so they can see the bigger picture.

You know what's really an underappreciated skill? Compass reading. More people should know how to navigate with a compass.

On one end of the spectrum, we have all the details, spelled out exactly, and at the other end of the spectrum, we have an approach that is pretty much all conceptual.

HOW DO YOU GIVE DIRECTIONS?

If mapping out someone's learning experience requires you to give direction, what's the best tactic for helping your learners get to their destinations?

STEP-BY-STEP DIRECTIONS

If you need to get your learners somewhere, you can just give them precise step-by-step directions throughout.

I give step-by-step instructions–the person just needs to follow them exactly, and they'll be fine.

Pros The learners are likely to be able to do the task pretty quickly by following the instructions.

Cons If something happens that falls outside of the directions, then the learner will be pretty much stuck.

Let's say you are giving someone driving directions—someone completely unfamiliar with the area where you live. You tell that person "Turn at the hair salon with the big purple sign," but the hair salon got taken over last week by a tattoo parlor who painted over the sign with a skull motif. Now your person is basically lost, and they don't have any way to self-correct because they don't have any concept of the big picture or any general sense of the neighborhood that will allow them to troubleshoot.

If it's too easy to follow the individual directions, then the learner won't learn.

When I'm driving in an unfamiliar city, I love my GPS device—it's much simpler than dealing with maps and directions, but it's not a good way to learn my way around a city. If I'm trying to get familiar with a new place, working from a map is much better. This goes back to the friction idea. A little extra effort can be useful for remembering.

The GPS is the low-friction choice. If you just want people to get there, exact instructions or a GPS are great (and that may be the best choice sometimes), but if you want people to learn how to get there, you want the process to be more effortful on the part of the learner.

DIY NAVIGATION

You can teach them all the concepts and principles they would need operate and troubleshoot.

Pros They'll really know how.

You can drop them in the middle of the Sonoran Desert and, given the basic tools, they'll be able to find their way out.

Cons It's overkill.

Unless you need people to understand at that level, you can choose a faster, more expedient method. It takes a long time to get people to understand the conceptual material at that level, and if you need to make them experts before they can do much with it, then it's probably not the most practical solution.

WAYFINDING—THE MIDDLE GROUND

Overall, it looks like the cons outweigh the pros in those two extremes. The answer is probably in the middle, between exact instructions and high-level concepts, because, remember, you don't only want your learners to be able to get where they're going, but you want other things for them as well:

- They should be able take what they've learned and apply it in multiple circumstances.
- They should be able to troubleshoot when things don't go quite as expected.
- They should have confidence about their ability to get where they are going.

APPLYING THE LEARNING IN MULTIPLE CIRCUMSTANCES

One of the biggest challenges when teaching skills is getting those skills to transfer to the real world, in multiple contexts.

Here's an example. A while ago I did a nifty little tutorial on how to make an envelope icon in PowerPoint (from the wonderful Rapid E-Learning Blog by Tom Kuhlmann, http://www.articulate.com/rapid-elearning).

This is what I created:

OK, it's not going to win any design awards, but for me it was a banner effort. And it made me wonder, based on this learning experience, how many other well-designed icons am I able to create?

Well, pretty much none. Zero, zip, zilch.

I created this with the tutorial equivalent of a GPS giving me turn-by-turn instructions. Left to my own devices, I simply don't know enough to apply this to other types of things. For example, I tried to make a coffee cup icon on my own, and this is what I came up with:

Not great. It pretty much looks like a roll of toilet paper with a handle.

So where did I go wrong? The problem wasn't with the tutorial, which did what it purported to do, in easy, clear steps. If all I needed to do was to make envelope icons, it would be more than sufficient.

There are some concepts and skills that I need before I will be able to create decent-looking icons without the aid of step-by-step instructions. For example, I probably need to know things like:

- How to determine the light source
- Where to add shadows and highlights
- How to layer gradients and transparencies
- How to make an interesting composition

Given that I don't know what I don't know, I'm probably missing some things on that list, too.

Working though a single example is not sufficient to teach me the necessary concepts. So, what's the best way to accomplish that?

OPTION 1: LOTS OF EXAMPLES

I could work through lots and lots of examples. Eventually, I would start to recognize patterns, and start to automatically do certain things that I'd repeated over and over.

This isn't the worst method, but it's probably a bit on the slow side, and it assumes that someone has created all the tutorials with step-by-step directions for a dozen or more other icons.

OPTION 2: CONCEPTS FOLLOWED BY EXAMPLES

The traditional method is to teach the concepts and then work on examples.

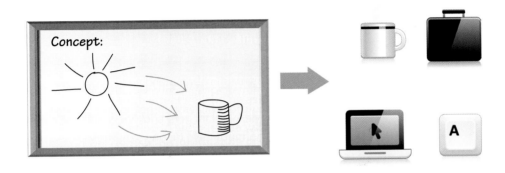

This is a reasonable approach, although you are asking your learners to understand the concepts without much up-front context.

OPTION 3: EXAMPLES FOLLOWED BY CONCEPTS

Let's say you have to drive to a destination that you've only been to once before. Are you more likely to remember how to get there if, on your previous visit, you:

a. drove yourself, or
b. were a passenger in the car?

There's a lot of benefit to letting learners drive themselves whenever possible.

One way to do so is to provide some examples, then let the learners help identify the concepts, rather than just telling them the concepts up front. After they've identified those concepts, they can apply them to additional examples. It could go something like this:

1. Work through some examples.
2. Have the students identify the concepts they saw in the examples.
3. Clarify the concepts and correct any misconceptions using the original examples as context.
4. Have the learners apply those concepts to further examples.

TROUBLESHOOTING

We've already talked about how another problem with step-by-step directions is that if learners steps off the path for any reason, they are pretty much, well, lost in the woods.

Unless they have prior knowledge to tap into, they don't really have any way to troubleshoot issues that don't run true to the given path.

One way to address that is to make sure that the learner has a higher-level sense of what's going on:

While making sure the learner knows about the big picture can be helpful, the other way to prepare learner to troubleshoot variations is somewhat counter-intuitive.

TELL THEM LESS, NOT MORE

Basically, if you want learners to be able to problem-solve and deal with variation, they need to practice doing just that. But, as we looked at in Chapter 5, examples that lay everything out in a logical order don't really require the learners to practice those skills.

You can give them that practice opportunity by leaving some holes in your examples that they need to figure out how to fill in, or by letting them know where they need to get to, but not all the details about how to get there.

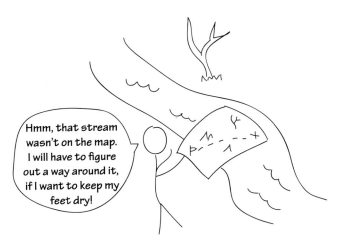

This is a little like having directions like "season to taste" in recipes. By having some gaps, rather than having only tidy, correct answers, learners are forced to figure out parts of the process themselves.

MAKE SURE THEY HAVE CONFIDENCE IN THEIR ABILITY

The best thing I got out of the envelope-icon tutorial (aside from a nifty envelope icon!) is the sense that I can, in the right circumstances, create something that doesn't look too bad.

While I was conscious at the time that those circumstances didn't add up to my being able to create those things without guidance, just the fact that I did it once meant that *it was possible*.

Ways for learners to gain confidence:

- **Have them do actual tasks, not just "activities based on the content."**
  If learners see some demonstrable evidence that they can actually *do*
  something with what they are learning, they'll be more likely to feel that way
  when they are trying to apply the knowledge later.
- **Make sure they have some early successes.** It's tempting to want to show
  them all the tricky, weird exceptions right off the bat, but it's good to start
  with tasks that will give learners early wins.
- **Let them work on their own problems.** Make sure that learners have the
  opportunity to take what they are learning and can apply it to real challenges
  in their own work or lives.
- **Let them drive themselves.** We talked about it above, but it bears repeating:
  Wherever possible, let learners drive themselves, rather than have them be
  passengers in your car.

In the book *What the Best College Teachers Do*, professor Donald Saari talks
about using a combination of stories and questions to challenge students to
think critically about calculus:

> *"When I finish the process...I want the students to feel like they have invented
> calculus and that only some accident of birth kept them from beating Newton
> to the punch."*

A PROCESS TO FOLLOW

A model I really like, and frequently use in my own design work, is Michael
Allen's CCAF model:

Context: The framework and conditions

Challenge: A stimulus to action within the context

Activity: A physical response to the challenge

Feedback: A reflection of the effectiveness of the learner's action

–From *Michael Allen's Guide to e-Learning*

Let's take a look at each of these steps in more detail, and at how each step
would play out in a learning design.

The scenario: You've been asked to create a training program for the SuperTech
customer service call center. SuperTech's latest smartphone product has some

interesting...er...features, and the customer service people have been getting hammered with irate customer calls.

In this case, the learners—those put-upon customer service reps (CSRs)—are supposed to use a three-step process (Validate, Diffuse, and Assist) when dealing with an irate customer.

STEP 1: DETERMINE CONTEXT

When I'm determining the context, I usually ask four questions:

- What is the general context for the task? For example, where does it come in the workflow, what is the purpose, and how often is it used?
- What is the emotional context for the task? For example, is the learner going to be under pressure or stress when they are using the knowledge? Are they going to be bored, or disrupted?
- What are the triggers that alert the learner that they will need to retrieve and use this knowledge? What's happening in their environment to let them know they need to do something?
- What is the physical context? Where are they, what objects are around them, and what or who are they interacting with?

If you got these answers to the questions, how would that impact your design for SuperTech?

- **General Context**—The CSRs get a variety of calls during the day. Most of these are run-of-the-mill calls. Irate calls have been increasing lately, but a CSR will still handle only 1–3 irate calls per shift, and depending on the shift, may have days without any irate calls.
  This helps you determine the interval. The CSRs may get two irate callers in a row, or may have an entire shift without any. Spreading out exposures to the material over time helps improve retention, which tells us we may want to have the training in chunks, spread out over a few days (we'll talk more about this in the next chapter).
- **Emotional Context**—CSRs operate in a fairly high-pressure environment. They are expected to meet calls-per-hour quotas, and they have to be knowledgeable about a wide variety of products. In the past, CSRs had the option of passing off highly irate customers to a supervisor, although they were encouraged to handle calls themselves if they could. With the increase in "hot" customer calls due to problems with SuperTech's new smartphone product, CSRs are increasingly required to handle the calls, and can pass

them to supervisors only if the caller demands a supervisor or becomes verbally abusive. CSRs are being pushed out of their comfort zone, and are feeling the stress of the unhappy customers, while continuing to have to meet their calls-per-hour goals despite the new situation.

We want the learners to become comfortable dealing with irate customers in a time-constrained environment while keeping calm themselves. Ideally, the training would mimic both the heightened emotional conditions and the time constraints. Learners could start with calmer, less time-constrained scenarios and the progress to more fraught, timed practice scenarios.

- **Triggers**—The customer's tone and wording are the cues that let the CSR know they are dealing with an irate caller.

  Part of the training should ensure that learners can recognize the signs or triggers that tell them they need to start using the validate / diffuse / assist process.

  In addition to practicing the "active" answers to the questions "is this an irate caller?" and "should I use the validate / diffuse / assist process with this caller?", the learner also needs to decide when they need to pass the caller on to a supervisor. These decisions points should be built into the challenge and activity.

- **Physical Context**—The CSR clicks a button on their computer screen to indicate they are available for a new call, which they receive over their telephone headset. They frequently get the customer's record on their computer screen, but sometimes have to search for the customer record. They have access to a screen that shows what product the customer has purchased, the history of their service plan, and the CSR notes from any previous customer calls.

  This tells you which artifacts—the customer records screens and telephone headsets—should be used as part of the training if possible. The physical context helps create cognitive associations that will help the learner retrieve the information as needed.

STEP 2: CHALLENGE

The question to ask yourself here is, what is an appropriate real-world challenge or accomplishment that the learner would do?

In our SuperTech case, a possible challenge could be satisfying or appropriately handling a certain number of customers.

STEP 3: WHAT'S THE ACTIVITY?

There are a number of ways to handle the activity portion of your learning design. Think about how you would set the activity for the learner to perform before you read the suggestions below.

DESIGN SUGGESTION: USE A PRE-ACTIVITY

Learners can be more prepared to learn if they have been primed ahead of time. Send an email out to ask the learners to collect a few irate customer problems, and a few possible solutions they've already been using ahead of time. Use these for scenarios or examples in the training (they can be sent to you as the learning designer or gathered in a central location like an intranet).

DESIGN SUGGESTION: CREATE E-LEARNING SCENARIOS

Depending on the size and geographic distribution of the audience, e-learning may be a practical solution. Create scenarios where learners need to use the validate / diffuse / assist process to lower the customer's heat level and successfully resolve the call.

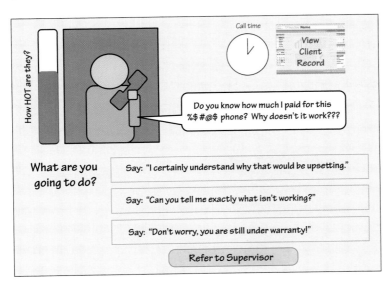

This design would need to have multiple scenarios, including a few that could be successfully resolved only by referring to the supervisor, and possibly one or two that didn't require the validate / diffuse / assist process because the customers weren't actually irate.

An effective way to get the learner started would be to have the first scenario be a walkthrough. Have you ever played a video game where the first level is heavily guided to introduce you to the game? A similar technique can be useful in e-learning. A first, untimed scenario could be a way to get familiar with the interface and with the validate / diffuse / assist process.

Ideally, the learners wouldn't do all the scenarios in one sitting. Instead, they would be spread out over a few days. For example, you could have the learner tackle three scenarios a day for three days. This way, the learner would have multiple exposures to the material, and the distribution would be closer to the distribution they would have in real life. Additionally, learners would have to refresh themselves on the validate / diffuse / assist process over multiple days, which would help consolidate their memory.

Keep in mind that this is only a *recognition* activity—unfacilitated e-learning is not a good medium for providing successful *recall* activities, because while computers can give quite good feedback on options that a learner selects, they aren't so adept at handling things the learner *recalls* (e.g., says or writes). So e-learning may be a reasonable way to learn about the validate / diffuse / assist process, but not as good a way to practice or develop the skills of using it.

Ugly Prototypes!

If the image on the previous page looks rough, and like something drawn quickly in PowerPoint, that's probably because it was. This is actually the kind of quick and dirty prototype that I would create for a client. A detailed look at production process for e-learning is beyond the scope of this book, but I strongly advocate for rapid prototyping as a way of sketching out designs. I typically don't spend a lot of time storyboarding the design before prototyping. As soon as we have the goals and audience and context defined, I'll start creating actual layouts and prototypes. There are different tools that can be used to prototype, but even PowerPoint can be used to create semi-functional prototypes by hyperlinking in the document.

DESIGN SUGGESTION: USE ROLE-PLAYS

It's going to be extremely difficult to try to simulate the emotional context of dealing with an irate customer without person-to-person role-plays. Because all the real-life interactions take place over the phone, the role-plays could take place in a classroom setting or even over the phone.

Role-plays can be done with the instructor or with other students. An instructor may be better at simulating an angry client, but using student-to-student role-plays can be a really practical way to give learners more practice opportunities.

As a starting point, you can give people a quick character sketch and talking points, and you can model a few role-plays in front of the whole group before having students work with each other. You also want to model critiquing the role-play, and give the students a structured feedback form, so they can evaluate together how well the process was followed.

DESIGN SUGGESTION: BLENDED LEARNING

If the scope of the project supports it, a combination of all the above strategies can be an effective way to address this problem from multiple perspectives and to make the most of the role-play activities by getting familiarization with validate / diffuse / assist out of the way using the e-learning scenarios to introduce the process. That way, learners can spend class time actively practicing, rather than listening to a description of the process.

DESIGN SUGGESTION: FOLLOW-UP ACTIVITIES AND JOB AIDS

The best way to support the continuation of a learned behavior is to give it some ongoing support. For example, you could distribute a take-away job aid that listed strategies for the validate / diffuse / assist process. Even better, give them a template, and have them create their own job aid so it will be more meaningful to them.

Additionally, follow-up e-learning scenarios could get sent out over the few weeks after the training, at the rate of one customer per week, to refresh learners on the process. There could be an intranet site with a discussion forum that allowed learners to document effective strategies and answers they used with irate clients. The best suggestions could be circulated via email to the whole audience. Any of these ideas would keep refreshing the process for the learners.

STEP 4: HOW ARE YOU GIVING THE LEARNER FEEDBACK?

Let's take a closer look at the details at some feedback options, bearing in mind that some feedback options are somewhat determined by the nature of the activity.

FEEDBACK IN THE E-LEARNING SCENARIO

There are a variety of ways the e-learning scenario can give feedback. There can be the client reaction, which can be not only what the client says, but the client's facial expression, and the client's tone of voice if audio is used. There can also be a "heat" meter that shows whether the client is getting calmer or hotter. These are all good ways to "show" rather than "tell." There can be more traditional "tell" feedback ("Good choice!") if absolutely necessary, but we want to leverage "showing" as much as possible. Ultimately the main source of feedback is the outcome—is the learner successful with the client? If not, they should probably have to try again until they are successful.

FEEDBACK IN THE ROLE-PLAYS

Feedback in face-to-face role-plays isn't as clear-cut as in an e-learning environment, because the learner isn't selecting from options and could say anything. However, there are some ways to structure the feedback to make it more effective:

- Have a feedback sheet that the "customer" or an observer could fill out, tracking how well the learner followed the process. The sheet could have a combination of checkboxes and short answer spaces so as to be quick to fill out, but also flexible.
- Use a similar feedback sheet to allow the learner to self-assess their own performance in the role-plays.
- The "customer" could have a set of "heat cards" which represented how irate they were supposed to be. As the learner effectively calms the customer, the customer could hand over heat cards, or could take them back if their "anger" level goes back up. If the learner can successfully get at least 80% of the cards, they would get credit for that customer.

ONGOING COACHING FEEDBACK

Ultimately, the best feedback would be ongoing coaching based on real perfor-mance. To do this, a supervisor could periodically listen in (a common practice in call centers) and provide detailed and specific feedback to the learner.

SUMMARY

- Use strategies like recall of prior knowledge and metacognition to help support memory encoding and retrieval.

- Some friction is necessary in learning. Just telling them is too smooth, and won't stick. Learners frequently need to engage with the material to retain it.

- Social interaction can be an effective way to add friction to learning.

- Whenever possible, show, don't tell.

- The right content is less than you think it is, has enough detail but no more, and is relevant to the learners.

- Starting with or using counter-examples can be a good way to prevent misconceptions.

- Decide how much guidance you need to give your learners. Resist the urge to hold their hand at every moment.

- A successful learning experience should leave the learner feeling confident and successful—"like they invented calculus."

- You can use CCAF (Context, Challenge, Activity, and Feedback) to design effective learning experiences.

REFERENCES

Bain, Ken. 2004. *What the Best College Teachers Do*. Cambridge: Harvard University Press.

Barrows, Howard S. 1996. Problem-based learning in medicine and beyond: A brief overview. *New Directions for Teaching and Learning, Bringing Problem-Based Learning to Higher Education: Theory and Practice, No. 68*. Wilkerson, Luann and Wim Gijselaers (Eds). San Francisco: Jossey-Bass.

Heath, Chip and Dan Heath. 2007. *Made to Stick: Why Some Ideas Survive and Others Die*. New York: Random House.

Kuperberg, Gina R, Balaji M. Lakshmanan, David N. Caplan, and Philip J. Holcomb. 2006. Making sense of discourse: An fMRI study of causal inferencing across sentences. *Neuroimage* 33: 343–361.

Moore, Cathy. 2011. Checklist for Strong Elearning. Cathy Moore: *Let's Save the World from Boring Elearning*. http://www.cathy-moore.com/resources/checklist-for-strong-elearning.pdf

Muller, D. A. 2008. Designing Effective Multimedia for Physics Education. PhD Thesis (School of Physics, University of Sydney).

Rich, Lani Diane and Alastair Stephens. 2011. Show And Tell, *Storywonk Daily*. http://storywonk.com/?p=210

DESIGN FOR SKILLS

(In which we learn that nobody wants to bike straight uphill all the time and if you don't give your learners chances to rest, they'll take them anyway)

DEVELOPING SKILLS

Teaching skills is not for the easily daunted. It takes time and effort and practice, both for you and for your learner.

In Chapter 1, we looked at the question you can use to determine if something is a skill:

> *Is it reasonable to think that someone can be proficient without practice?*

If the answer is no, it's not reasonable, then you know you are dealing with a skill.

Here's the thing. A lot of learning experiences purport to teach a skill, when really all they do is *introduce* the skill.

There's nothing wrong with introducing a learner to a skill, if that's the scope of your particular learning experience. If you've been given the task of creating a one-hour introduction to windsurfing or tamale-making or spreadsheet editing, then you are just introducing learners to that skill, and that's the scope of what you can do. An introduction familiarizes the learner with the skills, and that's a necessary first step.

But if you are actually trying to get your learners to some level of proficiency with a skill, then there's a little bit more involved.

There are two main components to developing a skill—**practice** and **feedback**.

PRACTICE

We've already addressed the fact that just handing a learner information doesn't make them proficient. A salesperson could have all the features of a product memorized, but that's only a tiny part of what makes them competent or skilled at their job.

Learners need to practice with the relevant skills and information before they can develop proficiency, but all too often, they just get a single dose of training on a topic or skill. For example, a salesperson might attend a 2-hour lecture on product features, with the expectation that that will be enough for salespeople to sell that product proficiently.

The truth is that anything that gets "learned" this way still gets put into long-term memory through practice. It just gets practiced on the job.

> Um, you need four-season shielding? OK... right...let me just look at the options, I know we have something that does that... I just, um, need... to...find it...

Either your give your learners the opportunity to practice, or they'll practice on their own. It might be a more painful process, and it might not be the kind of practice you want them to have...

In other words, you either create opportunities for learners to practice, or you take what you get.

STRUCTURING PRACTICE

So let's take a look at ways to structure practice. The goal of practice is eventually to get to proficiency and unconscious competence. Depending on the scope of your learning experience, that may or may not be a realistic goal, but we do want to move people along the path towards that.

WHAT HAPPENS TO YOUR BRAIN WHEN YOU ARE LEARNING SOMETHING NEW?

What's going on in your brain when you are learning something new? You're putting forth a lot of effort, and subsequently using a lot of glucose (the simple sugar that is one of the primary sources of energy in the body).

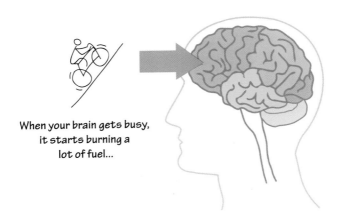

Basically, learning a lot of new information is the cognitive equivalent of biking uphill.

You make heavy use of areas of the brain like your frontal cortex (the rational reasoning concentration-y part of the brain). You can overload it pretty easily. Ever had the experience where you are taking in so much new information that your head kind of hurts?

HOW ABOUT WHEN YOU ARE USING SOMETHING YOU ALREADY KNOW?

When you are using learned behaviors, your brain runs much more efficiently, and uses less glucose.

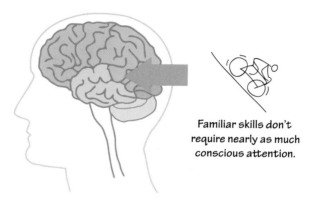

Familiar skills don't require nearly as much conscious attention.

When you're performing a familiar, learned behavior, it's more like the cognitive equivalent of coasting downhill.

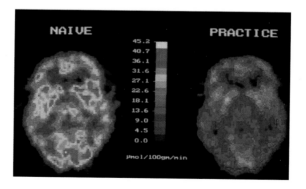

This image (Haier 1992) show how much glucose a brain burns when first learning how to play the video game Tetris (on the left) compared to the same brain after several weeks of practice (on the right). Even when playing a much harder level of Tetris, the practiced brain is likely to require significantly less energy.

HOW ARE LEARNING EXPERIENCES STRUCTURED?

Most learning experiences are structured around lots of new information.
Lots and *lots* of new information:

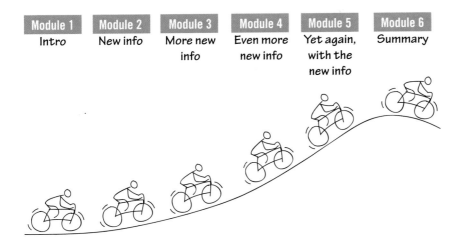

Module 1	Module 2	Module 3	Module 4	Module 5	Module 6
Intro	New info	More new info	Even more new info	Yet again, with the new info	Summary

The problem with this is that it's exhausting for your learners. Do you really
want to ask a new learner to bike straight uphill for the entire lesson? (Note:
Bicycling images are based on work I did at Allen Interactions, and are used
with their generous permission.)

How else could learning experiences be structured? An alternate structure for
learning would be to switch between these approaches, to allow the learner to
acclimate and assimilate the information before moving to the next level (inci-
dentally, this is how many games are structured).

Level 1	Level 2	Level 3	Level 4	Level 5	Level 6
Some new stuff, pretty easy, though	Stuff you know plus a bit more	Stuff you know, maybe a little faster	Stuff you know plus a bit more	Stuff you know, kicked up a notch	Boss Fight!

If the learner can't get up a part of the hill, they get to try again until they succeed. This ensures that the learner won't get into difficult territory until they are ready, and that they are staying at the edge of their ability level.

THIS IS A LOT LIKE FLOW

Have you ever been so engaged in an activity that you looked up and realized hours had passed, but it felt like only 15 minutes had gone by because you were so intensely engaged in what you were doing?

If so, you might have been experiencing what the Czech psychologist Mihaly Csikszentmihalyi called *flow*, which he describes as "joy, creativity, the process of total involvement with life."

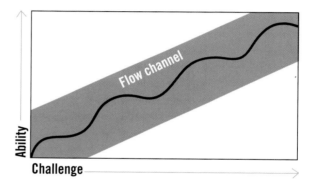

While Csikszentmihalyi's flow model has several aspects to it, one of the core tenets is a balance between ability and challenge.

When the challenge far exceeds a learner's ability, it's probably too difficult for that learner, and quickly becomes frustrating. But when something is far too easy for a learner, it's boring. On the other hand, something that is *slightly* too hard can be a satisfying challenge, while something that is a little bit easy can be a satisfying opportunity to coast for a few minutes.

Keeping people on that edge between challenge and ability is one of the fundamental principles of flow. Ideally, learning practice would allow learners a balance of challenge and satisfaction:

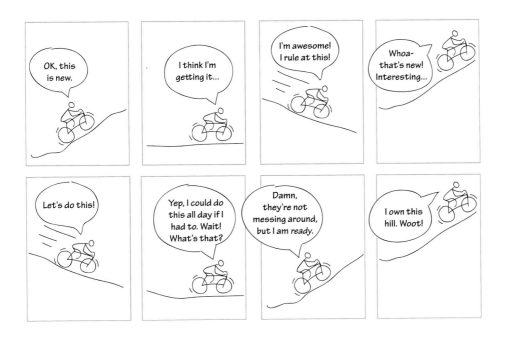

PAYING ATTENTION TO WHAT'S DIFFERENT

Another benefit of giving learners the opportunity to coast occasionally is that it allows them to pay attention to what's different.

When it's all new information, it's all uphill:

In the straight-uphill model, everything is new and everything is important, so therefore nothing is.

But when you balance the experience, the new material stands out:

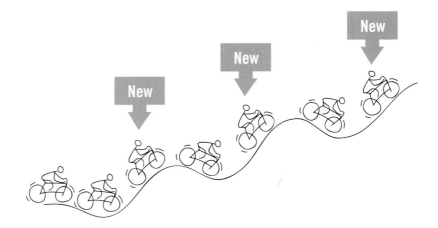

Not only does it stand out, but your learner has the energy to absorb it, and hasn't habituated to the influx of information.

And remember, if you don't give your learners breaks, they'll take them anyway:

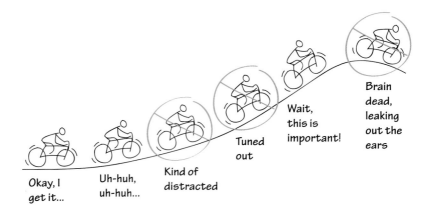

WHAT CAN THIS LOOK LIKE?

So how could this play out in practical terms? I worked with a client once that had a large team of sales/servicepeople. Their job had a steep learning curve, because there were technical aspects of how to fix machines with a very wide range of complicated products. The client considered the employees to be salespeople first, and servicepeople second, so they were very interested in improving sales skills. Also, the sales/servicepeople were expected to run their territories like their own business, and required the skills and knowledge to do that.

The client wanted to add e-learning to their curriculum, because the current training for new hires consisted of a two-week class at the main office where they basically tried to give the learners as much information as they could possibly absorb, followed by some job-shadowing and some feedback ride-alongs with their managers.

So, it's no wonder the client wanted to add e-learning to their curriculum. What they were doing was basically like biking straight uphill for two weeks without a break. Learners were effectively being asked to jam five years' worth of clothing into a space the size of a gym locker. As you can imagine, they had a tough time taking everything in, and an even tougher time retaining it. As a result, many learned on the job in hit-or-miss fashion. It's a testament to the strong culture of the organization that the ones who survived often did quite well, but the client felt they could do better, and wanted a curriculum that did a better job of developing skills over time.

The revised curriculum looked like this:

- An initial in-person class shortened to a few days
- Job-shadowing with an experienced employee
- The remainder of the curriculum spread out over two dozen simulated sales calls intended to be completed within 2–3 months
- Follow-up assignments to be performed in the field based on the content learned in each e-learning module
- A field assessment system that had checklists of all the crucial competencies (technical, product, sales, etc.), with which managers verified that the learners could actually do all the necessary tasks
- Follow-up or reinforcement classes as needed

This program didn't require the learner to try to grasp all the information all at once. Instead it was spread out over time. By the time the learner finished the last few e-learning models, they already had a few months of experience to provide context.

Then managers, using the field assessment system, could figure out pretty quickly where there were gaps, and use review of the relevant e-learning lesson and face-to-face coaching to try to address those gaps. The revised program was able to provide feedback loops to help verify and improve competencies.

SPACING OUT THE PRACTICE OVER TIME

How many times does someone need to practice something, and how often?

Think about the following example:

You are a recycling coordinator for your medium-sized town, and part of your job is to educate the public about how to sort their recycling.

Most of the folks are pretty environmentally oriented, so you don't have much trouble getting people to go through your recycling training classes, but you are noticing that people just aren't following through.

They do a good job the first time they recycle after the class, but after that they pretty quickly forget the right things to do. Part of the problem is that recycling for common materials (paper, cans, and glass) happens only every two weeks, and recycling for less common items (some plastics, batteries, etc.) happens only once a month. Most of your issues are with the less common items.

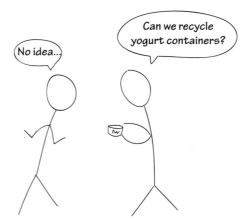

You consider a few options for how to correct this problem:

- You could add an extra 30 minutes to the class so people could get extra hands-on recycling practice and *really* learn the behavior.
- You could do a follow-up email every day for two weeks, with an online link to a recycling practice game, where people could practice what they learned.
- You could send the online link for the recycling practice game once a month for the next year.

If you could choose only one option for maximum long-term retention, which option do you think would work the best?

This is actually a pretty well-researched question. Basically, is practice better if it's all massed together or if it's distributed over time?

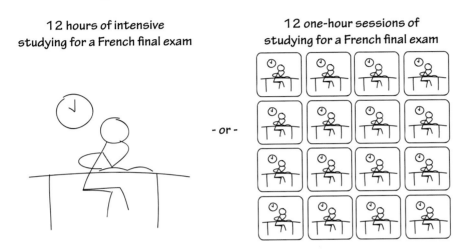

| 12 hours of intensive studying for a French final exam | 12 one-hour sessions of studying for a French final exam |

- or -

The answer depends somewhat on what's being studied, but for the most part, **you want to distribute your learning over time if possible**.

The first time you learn something, you obviously want to spend enough time to ensure you have a good grasp on the material, but extra practice **at that time** will provide a diminishing return.

HOW LONG SHOULD YOU WAIT?

Somewhat counter-intuitively, a longer period in between practice sessions can lead to longer overall retention. A good general rule of thumb is to time the practices to how often you'll need to use the behavior.

Say you are teaching your Aunt Joan how to attach pictures to her emails and you want her to *really* learn it so she stops making you come over once or twice a week to do it for her. How often would you want Aunt Joan to practice?

You would probably have her practice the task 1–2 times a week until she is able to competently do it herself, to match how frequently she is going to retrieve and use the knowledge later.

If that's not practical (Uncle Carlos has the same problem, but is only going to be in town for a week), then you want, at a minimum, to at least spread the practice over several days. There seems to be a benefit in sleeping between learning reinforcements. The act of sleeping seems to help consolidate what people learn, so having practice over multiple days takes advantage of that phenomenon.

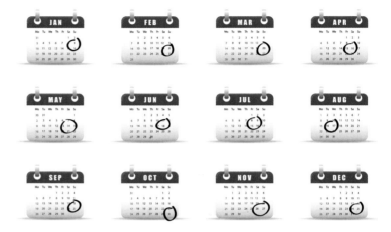

The best choice for the recycling training would be a reminder once a month, since it was the monthly recycling items that were posing the biggest problems for the learners. Additionally, if you could time the reminder to come a day or two before the particular learner's recycling date, the practice exercise would also act as a job or a reference that a person could consult if unsure.

FEEDBACK

In order for practice to be effective, learners need to be able to tell how they are doing. This is particularly important for skill development, because practicing something incorrectly can be worse than not practicing at all. The incorrect skill can become ingrained, and then correcting that skill later will require unlearning behaviors that have become automatic.

We looked at some of the characteristics of good feedback in the previous chapter (e.g., show don't tell, consequence-based feedback), but there are a few other considerations that you may want to think about when providing feedback for practice and skill development.

FREQUENCY OF FEEDBACK

If you've ever played video games, you were probably thinking "Wow! Look at the corrective feedback mechanisms for shaping behavior that are in this game!"

OK, you probably *weren't* thinking that, but if you were, award yourself a learning-nerd power-up.

I bring up games again because they are fantastic little laboratories of skill development, and a big part of why games are so good at developing skills is the frequency and variety of feedback mechanisms. Most modern video games give the player feedback every few seconds. Even a slower game will give feedback every few minutes.

So how often do (non-video-game) learners typically get feedback? A worst-case scenario might be the college lecture class that has two grades—the midterm and the final. A student could be veering off course for *months* before getting any course correction.

The good news is that if you use the Context, Challenge, Activity, and Feedback model, or if you design a curriculum around structured goals, you have lots of built-in feedback points. You should look for opportunities to increase the frequency of feedback whenever possible.

VARIETY OF FEEDBACK

Let's say that video game you play has the immediate goal of killing as many zombies as possible. And let's say that every time you killed a zombie, a pop-up box appeared that said "Good Job. You successfully killed a zombie! Click the Continue button to continue!"

I'd call that a candidate for Worst Game Ever at that point.

Increasing the frequency of feedback is great, but if you do that, you also want to have *various ways* to provide feedback.

If we look at games again, we see that video games use feedback devices like sounds, points, character reactions, scores, and visual cues. Live games like board games or kids' games also have feedback mechanisms that don't involve slamming the action to a halt and explicating or stating something. In Monopoly, you don't get lectured about poor business choices—you lose money, or go bankrupt, or go to jail.

FOLLOW-UP COACHING

The feedback that happens after the learning experience is over should be like good coaching. It helps the learner understand where they are doing things right, where they are doing things wrong, and what they should try instead.

Frequency matters here as well. The typical workplace format is to give performance reviews on an annual basis. How useful do you think that is for shaping behaviors?

Yeah, frequently not at all. Providing coaching and feedback only on an annual basis is like predicting the weather, where the further out it goes, the more inaccurate it gets.

Figuring out when the check-ins need to occur can be enormously helpful. Part of designing your learning experience should be setting a schedule.

- When are you going to follow up?
- What will be evaluated?
- What criteria will be used?

This gives learners an opportunity to head for the goal.

> **Specific Criteria** Make your feedback extra-helpful by using explicit, standardized criteria. A feedback sheet or checklist can also make it feasible for the learner to self-assess, which can be useful both for practical considerations and in keeping the learner aware of the criteria.

OTHER WAYS TO FOLLOW UP

If the structure and setup of your learning situation doesn't allow for coaching follow-up, there are other ways to reach out and follow up with learners.

- Create a forum online and encourage learners to report back on their experiences.
- Send periodic emails with examples, tips, and opportunities for learners to self-evaluate.
- Have virtual critique sessions that allow learners to post work and get feedback from the community.

A word about assessment

There's a whole science behind assessment that's beyond the scope of this book, but I did want to address a few issues.

Arguably the most common form of formal assessment is everybody's favorite—the multiple-choice question! We've all answered more multiple-choice questions that we can possibly remember.

Why are these tests so darn popular? Well, they have a few main advantages:

- They are efficient to write, administer, and score.
- Grading is objective.
- They are consistent; everyone who takes the test can have essentially the same experience.

OK, so what ISN'T on that list? Oh yeah—there's pretty much nothing on there about the learning advantages for the person taking the test.

Multiple-choice tests aren't really about making the learner better at what they need to do. They are about making test administration efficient and consistent. If your main goal is testing and assessment, then that's fine. You've got yourself a model.

But here's the thing. Mainly what you learn from multiple-choice tests is how good the learner is at taking...multiple-choice tests. You don't want to hand someone the keys to the helicopter just because they passed the 100-question multiple-choice test on the history of helicopter flight.

If your main goal is coaching the learner and assessing competency, throw out your snazzy slick multiple-choice questions; they aren't going to help much. Instead, do these two things:

- Have the learner perform the task
- Give them useful feedback

That's it.

DESIGN FOR ACCOMPLISHMENTS

So let's take a look at an example. Remember Todd, our new restaurant manager? You are creating a new version of a course to train Todd and other new restaurant managers. Your target audience are folks who have a fair amount of restaurant experience in other capacities (servers, kitchen staff, etc.) who are moving into management roles.

The course is supposed to cover everything from the basic elements (e.g., how to verify employee timesheets) all the way up to high-level strategy thinking about the restaurant as a business (e.g., the market position of the restaurant).

The old course is a series of modules:

- Hiring
- Managing staff
- Safety
- Employment procedures
- Ordering and inventory
- Bar and beverage sales
- Restaurant financials
- Customer service
- Presentation
- Health and quality control
- Marketing and promotion

The old course has pretty good content in it, but the students seem to be struggling on the job. Even if they did well in the course, they don't remember a lot of the information once they started work, and they have a hard time applying a lot of the information when they do remember it. Most eventually learn what they need to know, although a lot wash out along with the way, which is a waste of time and money. Most of them also continue to struggle with taking the strategic view, even after they've figured out the day-to-day stuff.

We discussed the necessity for repetition and practice if you want to develop skills, but the current course structure doesn't allow for that. Once a learner finishes with the Safety module, they don't revisit it, even though the ability to spot safety violations as soon as they occur is an important skill for managers.

In restructuring the restaurant-manager course, you want the students to actually develop the necessary skills, and be more ready to hit the ground running when they get on the job. You want the course to help develop skills, not just deliver information. How could you restructure the course to give the learners a chance to practice more, and to have multiple exposures to different items? Let's take a look at one possibility that uses a structure based on games.

HOW GAMES ARE STRUCTURED

We want to build skills and expertise, and we've already talked a little about how games are really good at this, but let's take a closer look at how games do this.

James Paul Gee, a scholar who studies video games for learning, describes it this way:

> Expertise is formed in any area by repeated cycles of learners practicing skills until they are nearly automatic, then having those skills fail in ways that cause the learners to have to think again and learn anew. Then they practice this new skill set to an automatic level of mastery only to see it, too, eventually be challenged.

> Good games create and support the cycle of expertise, with cycles of extended practice, tests of mastery of that practice, then a new challenge, and then new extended practice. This is, in fact, part of what constitutes good pacing in a game (Gee 2004).

One of the ways that games structure these cycles of expertise is by having immediate, short-term, medium-term, and long-term accomplishments for the learner.

So, for example, in the video game Diner Dash, you play the character of Flo, a waitress. Your immediate goals are to seat people, take orders, deliver food, and clear tables. Your short-term goal is to successfully complete a shift in the diner. Your medium-term goal is to upgrade to a better restaurant. Your long-term goal is to win the game. If you fail at lower goals, you can't move on to higher goals, and you have to practice until you are proficient enough to succeed.

Sebastian Deterding, a games researcher, uses this graphic to show a structured flow of goals (Deterding 2011):

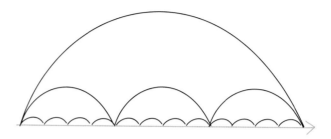

The accomplishment of short-term goals are necessary to achieve the longer-term goals, which in turn roll up to accomplish the overarching goals.

If you were using this structure for a sales course, you might have this as your set of goals:

Timeframe	Goal
Immediate goal	Gather relevant data about different customers and their needs
Short-term goal	Determine a product and sales approach for different clients based on their needs
Medium-term goal	Succeed in closing with the client (make the sale, get the meeting, get the referral)
Long-term goal	Hit your sales quota for the quarter and win a trip to Hawaii

So instead of having a sales course that's structured with a module about determining customer needs, followed by a module product features and benefits, followed by a module about the sales process with the client, you have a series of goals, and if you fail at any goal, you have to practice and try again until you succeed.

Another course I've seen this applied to taught police officers how to recognize possible warning signs for terrorism (Allen Interactions 2010):

Timeframe	Goal
Immediate goal	Gather relevant data at different incident sites
Short-term goal	Determine if an individual incident needed to be reported, and if so, what data supported that conclusion
Medium-term goal	Successfully complete a day on patrol after investigating 2-4 incidents
Long-term goal	Head off the terrorist attack

There are a couple of big benefits to this way of structuring a learning experience:

- Learners are practicing the actual behaviors that they need to perform in the real world.
- Learners don't progress until they can master the necessary elements.
- Learners get multiple exposures to the concepts and material, and develop increasing proficiency with those multiple exposures.
- Learners can have some success in the environment, because they can almost always achieve some of the goals, but get specific feedback.
- Increasing levels of challenge, and new goals to pursue, keep the learner engaged.

HOW TO USE THIS FOR LEARNING

So let's go back to our restaurant management course.

How could you structure the course differently using short-term, medium-term, and long-term goals? Consider your answer before looking at one possible design solution outlined below.

Timeframe	Goal
Immediate goal	Respond to specific challenges that happen during a shift (late employee, unhappy customer, paperwork, cashing out, safety issues, etc.)
Short-term goal	Successfully complete a dinner shift
Medium-term goal	Successfully complete a full week, including financials, inventory, ordering, employees issues, etc.
Long-term goal	Successfully complete a quarter, including hiring, menu planning, marketing, and strategic planning for the next quarter

In this scenario, the learner could focus on the immediate skills needed to survive a restaurant shift first, such as supervising employees, paperwork, dealing with an inventory shortage, etc.

Then the learner could step back and focus on the skills for managing the restaurant for a week, such as scheduling, longer-term employee issues, inventory, and financials.

After that, the learner could focus on the skills necessary to manage the restaurant longer term—quarterly planning, hiring, team-building, marketing, menu planning, and ordering.

This way, instead of learning all about one topic in a single sitting, and then moving on to the next topic, they would get multiple exposures to a topic over time. For example, you could address safety in a specific incident at the shift level, in preparing for an inspection at the week level, and in improving safety records at the quarterly level. That way, the topic of safety would be addressed multiple times over the entire course.

Always being able to see the next goal, and knowing what you need to work on next, is another characteristic of Csikszentmihalyi's flow model.

Let's say you've signed up to run a marathon, and when you check in to pick up your number, the organizer tells you that it's a free-form marathon, and that you should just start running due west, and that after 26 miles, you'll find the finish line.

"Exactly 26 miles, due west" is an exact destination, but it's not a very satisfying one, because you won't know if you are on course or not, or how much progress you're making. Your learners want to know where they need to head to next, and they want feedback on how they are doing while getting there.

SUMMARY

- Teaching skills requires two main elements—practice and feedback.

- Learners will practice with you or without you, but you may not like what they are practicing when they do it without you.

- Brain function gets more efficient with practice.

- Avoid a steady stream of new information—it's exhausting to your learners. Instead, build in opportunities for your learners to get a little proficiency with the new information before you move to the next element.

- If you don't give your learners a chance to rest, they'll take it anyway.

- Flow is a state of engagement that can be created through a balance of challenge and ability.

- Space practice out over time.

- Promote engagement by using structured goals and real accomplishments.

- Use frequent and multifaceted feedback to shape behavior.

- When assessing learner performance, have them perform the actual task whenever possible.

REFERENCES

Allen Interactions. 2010. *Custom e-learning: Allen Interactions—Law Enforcement Response to Terrorism. http://www.youtube.com/watch?v=Vt8xkOTqwjg*

Csikszentmihalyi, Mihaly. 1990. *Flow: The Psychology of Optimal Experience.* New York: Harper.

Deterding, Sebastian. 2011. Don't Play Games With Me! Presentation on slideshare.net; http://www.slideshare.net/dings/dont-play-games-with-me-promises-and-pitfalls-of-gameful-design?from=ss_embed, slide 63.

Gee, James Paul. 2004. Learning by Design: Games as Learning Machines. *Gamasutra Magazine,* http://www.gamasutra.com/gdc2004/features/20040324/gee_01.shtml.

Haier, R.J., B.V. Siegel Jr., A. MacLachlan, E. Soderling, S. Lottenberg, and M.S. Buchsbaum. 1992 Regional glucose metabolic changes after learning a complex visuospatial/motor task: a positron emission tomographic study. *Brain Research* 570: 134–14.

Karpicke, Jeffrey D. and Janell R. Blunt. 2011. Retrieval Practice Produces More Learning than Elaborative Studying with Concept Mapping. *Science,* DOI:10.1126/science.1199327.

Thalheimer, Will. 2006. Spacing Learning Events Over Time. From *Work-Learning Research, Inc.,* http://www.work-learning.com/catalog.

Zeleny, Milan. 1987, Management Support Systems: Towards Integrated Knowledge Management. *Human Systems Management* 7(1): 59-70.

DESIGN FOR MOTIVATION

(In which we learn that we don't always learn
the right thing when we learn from experience,
and that the elephant is a creature of habit)

There are two main types of motivation that we concern ourselves
with as learning designers:

- Motivation to *learn*
- Motivation to *do*

We've already spent a lot of time looking at motivation to learn
(remember the elephant?), so this chapter is going to concern itself
with motivation to *do*.

MOTIVATION TO DO

Numerous studies have come out in the last few years that say texting
while driving is a very very dangerous thing to do.

Shocking.

That texting while driving is dangerous probably isn't a surprise to the
vast majority of the population. So why do people continue to do it?
I don't know exactly, but I suspect it's because people have one, or a
mix, of the following thoughts and responses:

- *"I know it's a bad idea, and I never do it (except when I do, and
  then I feel guilty)."*
- *"I know it's a bad idea, but I only do it once in a while, and I'm
  very careful."*

- *"I know it's a bad idea for other people, but I can do it because I'm really good at it."*
- *"Huh? What's the big deal?"*

Most of the responses above indicate that this is not a knowledge problem, and that an intervention that focuses on knowledge isn't going to change anything, because it's not the "know" part but rather the "do" part of the sentence that's the problem.

So why do people *do* things they *know* are a bad idea? It's not because they aren't smart people.

A big part of this goes back to our elephant and rider. Frequently, the rider *knows*, but the elephant still *does*.

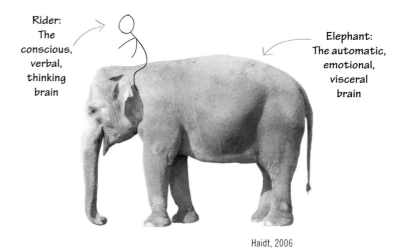

Rider:
The conscious, verbal, thinking brain

Elephant:
The automatic, emotional, visceral brain

Haidt, 2006

WE LEARN FROM EXPERIENCE

Part of the reason for "I *know*, but..." is that people learn from *experience*, which is a great thing (we wouldn't want to live in a world where people didn't), but it can cause some problems. The elephant in particular can be far more influenced by experience than by abstract knowledge.

Here's an example. Let's say that 1 in 10 instances of texting while driving results in an accident (this isn't a real statistic; I don't think that exact data is known—this is just for purposes of argument). Let's take a look at the experience of two different drivers:

Texting while driving

	Driver 1	Driver 2
1st Time	OK	OK
2nd Time	Has nasty fender bender	OK
3rd Time	Doesn't text	OK
4th Time	Doesn't text	OK
5th Time	Doesn't text	OK
6th Time	Doesn't text	OK
7th Time	Doesn't text	OK
8th Time	Doesn't text	OK
9th Time	Doesn't text	OK
10th Time	Doesn't text	Has an accident

Both drivers are learning from experience, but the lesson Driver 2 is learning from experience is that texting while driving is *fine*—see, look at all the experience that confirms that! Until it isn't fine, of course.

This is why people have a really hard time with activities where the action is now but the consequence is later. The elephant is a creature of immediacy. Take a look at these classic "I know, but..." activities.

Classic "I know, but..." activities

Activity	Immediate Consequence	Delayed Consequence
Smoking	Nice nicotine hit	Lung cancer
Saving for retirement	Less money	More money
Exercise	Ouch	Nice abs!
Doughnuts	Mmm...	I'm not getting on that scale...

In these activities, the elephant is being asked to sacrifice in the present for some future gain, but the elephant is only really persuaded by what's happening now, and by the experience of the immediate consequences. The rider knows that there's an association with the future consequence, but whatever that future consequence is, it's too abstract to influence the elephant.

REMEMBER, CHANGE IS HARD

Now, you might not be trying to fix behaviors as difficult as smoking, but anything that involves extra effort is going to be a lot easier if the elephant is on board with the program.

In particular, changing an existing pattern of behavior can require effort for the elephant. The elephant is a creature of habit, which means that if the elephant is used to going left, it's going to require a fair bit of conscious effort to get it to go right instead.

Before we look at ways to influence learner behavior, and while this word "change" keeps popping up, let's be clear on one thing: none of this is about *controlling* the learner. It's not about tricking your learners into compliance. Instead, it's about designing environments that make it easier for those learners to succeed.

The experience they have when they are learning about something can make a difference in the decisions they make later.

DESIGNING FOR BEHAVIOR

Let's take a look at some methods to design for behavior change or reinforcement.

THE TECHNOLOGY ACCEPTANCE MODEL (TAM)

The technology acceptance model (Davis 1989) is an information systems model that looks at what variables affect whether or not someone adopts a new technology. It's been fairly well researched, and although it isn't without its critics, I find it to be a useful frame. At the heart of the model are two variables:

Perceived Usefulness	Perceived Ease of Use
Does the learner see this change as something that will be useful to them?	Does the learner see this change as something that will be easy to use or implement?

It's not a complicated idea—if you want someone to use something, they need to believe that it's actually useful, and that it won't be a major pain in the ass to use.

TAM specifically addresses technology adoption, but those variables make sense in a lot of other areas as well. You want someone to use a new method of coaching employees? Or maybe a new safety procedure? If your audience believes that it's pointless (i.e., not useful) or it's going to be a major pain (i.e., not easy to use), they will probably figure out ways around it. Then it either fails to get adopted or you get into all sorts of issues around punishments or incentives to try to force the change to happen.

I keep TAM in mind when I design anything that requires adopting a new technology or system or practice (which is almost everything I do). Some of the questions I ask are:

- **Is the new behavior genuinely useful?** Sometimes it's *not* useful for the learner, but it is useful for the organization, or it's a compliance necessity. In those cases, it can be a good idea to acknowledge it and make sure the learner understands why the change is being made—that it isn't just the organization messing with their workflow, but that it's a necessary change for other reasons.
- **If it is useful, how will the learner know that?** You can cite case studies, examples, people talking about how it's helped them, or give the learner the experience of it being useful through simulations. Show Don't Tell becomes particularly important here. You can assert usefulness until you're blue in the face, and you won't get nearly as much buy-in as you will if learners are able to try it, or to hear positive endorsements from trusted peers. Can you involve learners in planning the change so they can have input and can help make sure that the change will be effective?

- **Is the new behavior easy to use?** If not, why not? Is it too complex? Is it because people are too used to their current system? People will learn to use even the most hideous system by mentally automating tasks, but then when you ask them to change, it's really difficult because they can no longer use those mental shortcuts, and the new system feels uncomfortably effortful until they've had enough practice.
- **If it's not easy to use, is there anything that can be done to help that?** Can the learners practice enough to make it easier? Can you make job aids or other performance supports? Can you roll it out in parts so they don't have to tackle it all at once? Can you improve the process or interface to address ease-of-use issues?

DIFFUSIONS OF INNOVATION

The other model I find really useful is from Everett Rogers' classic book *Diffusion of Innovations*. If you haven't read it, you might want to get a copy. It's a really entertaining read, packed with intriguing case studies and loaded with useful stuff. The part I want to focus on here is his take on what perceived attributes affect whether a user adopts or rejects an innovation:

Relative Advantage—The degree to which an innovation is perceived as being better than the idea it supersedes

Compatibility—The degree to which an innovation is perceived to be consistent with the existing values, past experiences, and needs of potential adopters

Complexity—The degree to which an innovation is perceived as difficult to use

Observability—The degree to which the results of an innovation are visible to others

Trialability—The opportunity to experiment with the innovation on a limited basis (Rogers 1983)

There is obviously some crossover with TAM, but if I'm designing a learning experience for a new system, I use this as a mental checklist:

- Are the learners going to believe the new system is better?
- Are there compatibility issues that need to be addressed?
- Can we do anything to reduce complexity?
- Do the learners have a chance to see it being used?
- Do the learners have a chance to try it out themselves?
- How can learners have the opportunity to have some success with the new system?

If somebody really, *really* doesn't want to do something, designing instruction around these elements probably isn't going to change their mind. And if a new system, process, or idea is really sucky, or a pain in the ass to implement, then it's going to fail no matter how many opportunities you give the learner to try it out.

How might this play out in a real-life, on-the-job situation? Let's say you are responsible for creating training for a network of nursing homes. There have been a number of incidents lately with residents falling down and injuring themselves. The network has started a new initiative to try to reduce the number of falls. Your job is to train the staff to use a new process for evaluating a resident's risk level for falling. The staff is supposed to use a five-point checklist (steadiness, use of walking aids, physical dexterity, vision impairment, and environmental hazards) to evaluate a resident's risk, and to take action on high-risk ratings. The difficulty is that this is a different procedure than has been used in the past, and it is extra work for the already busy staff.

What could you build into a learning experience for each of the check-points to make it more likely that the staff will use the new procedure?

Think about each of Everett's attributes (relative advantage, compatibility, complexity, observability and trialability), and how you accomplish each of these for the new procedure. Consider how you would apply these ideas before reading the design suggestions below.

Design suggestions:

- **Relative Advantage** Is there a way for the user to see how many more falls can be prevented using the new system? This can be done with statistics, but statistics talk to the rider, not the elephant. Some way to make this information more visceral for people will have more impact.

  For example, learners might be able to identify with the story of Millie, a lively resident who is negatively affected by a fall, and has to struggle to come back. The new method can be used to prevent Millie from falling again.

  Statistics can also be translated into tangibles. For example, a 17% reduction in falls can mean X more residents who can visit their families for the holidays and Y more residents who can operate independently, which ultimately equals less work for the staff also.

  Another way to show relative advantage would be for the learners to work through a few cases using the old system, and then assessing those same cases using the new system. They can then report back on how many more potential hazards were identified using the new system. By having the learners discover and report back on the advantages, it becomes more Show than Tell.

- **Compatibility** One way to improve compatibility is to recruit the learners on this task. As part of the training, have them look at how this new procedure is incompatible, and then have them help brainstorm ways to make it more compatible with the existing process.

- **Complexity** The first step in clarifying and taming complexity is to reduce the learners' perceived *sense* of complexity by giving them enough opportunities to practice such that the process starts to feel easier to them.

   The second step is to actually reduce the complexity. If the new process adds a separate form, can it be incorporated with the existing forms? If it's a situation where the learners have to write notes, can some of the items be converted to a checklist so they don't have to remember as much, and so they can fill out the documentation faster?

- **Observability** Are there pilot programs that the learner can observe? Can you identify opinion leaders (the folks everybody listens to) and have them use the new process first, so everyone else can see how it's going?

- **Trialability** Stage some practice scenarios that the learners can work through to see how the new system works. After they've had a chance to try it out, regroup and smooth out any rough edges, questions, or issues with the learners.

SELF-EFFICACY

Self-efficacy can be described as someone's belief in their own ability to succeed. Basically, it's the little engine that could ("I think I can...I think I can...").

Which of these guys do you think is going to be more likely to try a new method or procedure?

Earlier in the book, I mentioned a curriculum for drug and alcohol prevention for middle-school students (www.projectalert.com). One of the key elements of that curriculum is developing the students' sense of *resistance self-efficacy.*

Dealing with peer pressure involving drugs, cigarettes, and alcohol is another classic "I know, but..." scenario, right? For example, kids don't start smoking because they don't know smoking is bad. They've all gotten that message, so there are other reasons. But the situations where students need to make the right decision are emotionally fraught, high-stress situations. Being able to act confidently can make a big difference in those situations.

Students participating in the prevention curriculum practice, and practice more, and practice *more* how they are going to handle the situation. They have statements ready, and they've tried them out in role-play scenarios. Additionally, they have the confidence of their peer group in the class, who have also talked about their strategies in the same circumstances.

In addition to feeling capable, it helps if learners also feel that the necessary task or skill is within their control.

Carol Dweck, a social and developmental psychologist and researcher, conducted an experiment with fifth graders (Mueller & Dweck 1998). She had the students solve a set of problems. When they were done, half the group was told "You must be smart at these problems" and the others were praised for their effort—"You must have worked hard at these problems." They then had students attempt subsequent tasks.

Dweck describes the results:

> We found that praise for intelligence tended to put students in a fixed mind-set (intelligence is fixed, and you have it), whereas praise for effort tended to put them in a growth mind-set (you're developing these skills because you're working hard). We then offered students a chance to work on either a challenging task that they could learn from or an easy one that ensured error-free performance. Most of those praised for intelligence wanted the easy task, whereas most of those praised for effort wanted the challenging task and the opportunity to learn.

When the students tackled subsequent tasks, the students who had been praised for intelligence (something not in their control) did worse than they had done initially, and the students who had been praised for working hard (something they *did* control) did better overall.

Well, that seems to have worked pretty effectively with kids, but are there ways to improve the self-efficacy of adult learners as well?

Let's revisit Marianna, from Chapter 1. You'll recall that she is a newly minted supervisor for her company's IT support department. She was a great IT support person and now she's been promoted, supervising five other IT support workers.

Her HR department has sent her to a new-manager training class, where she learned all about the paperwork necessary for managing hourly workers, and about a coaching model for providing good and timely feedback to her direct reports.

Marianna's first few weeks have been a bit rocky. She is swamped by the paperwork demands, and has to work really hard to keep up. Other supervisors seem to stay on top of their paperwork, so Marianna isn't really sure what she's doing wrong. A couple of her employees are starting to come in late, and she's reluctant to confront them directly about it, because she doesn't want it to seem like she got all bossy just because she was promoted. She tries to use the coaching method she was taught, but while it works a little with one of the problem employees, it doesn't work at all with the other, and as Marianna gets busy, she doesn't really finish all the steps to the coaching process. She's not that convinced it was helpful, anyway.

Marianna's manager is aware that she's struggling somewhat, and is thinking of arranging more managerial training for her.

What are some ways you could design learning experiences that would increase Marianna's sense of self-efficacy? Think about your own answer before reading the design suggestion that follows.

Design suggestion → Practice is a really good place to start, probably first through role-playing with her supervisor, or with others who can give her good feedback. She can also shadow some other supervisors who are successfully using the coaching model, and see it in use. She can try using the coaching model for smaller issues, rather than using it to tackle major performance problems right out of the gate. If she can use it to solve some smaller issues, she can gain more confidence in using it with bigger, more intimidating issues. Additionally, she can practice establishing herself as the supervisor of the team by doing some other activities that are non-punitive—possibly ones around developing the team in positive ways. This will make her more confident in her role as supervisor, which will help when it comes time to deal with more challenging issues.

MODELING AND PRACTICE

In Marianna's example, we looked at the value of observing someone else, and of practicing to develop self-efficacy.

These practices have other benefits besides developing self-efficacy. We know that the elephant is a creature of habit, and that it likes to learn from its direct experience (remember the second driver in the texting example?).

Well-worn path

It takes effort to switch paths. By creating opportunities for the learner to see behaviors modeled and to practice them, you greatly increase the likelihood that those behaviors will continue later. A particularly useful resource on creating new, positive habits is the work of BJ Fogg (www.behaviormodel.org).

Another way to practice and to help increase the likelihood of a behavior being used is to walk learners a few steps down the path as part of the learning design. By this I mean, have your learners prepare themselves to employ the knowledge or skill by actively figuring out how they will use it to address their own specific challenges or tasks—stick with them as they think through moving from the theoretical to the practical.

We've talked a lot about using scenarios to make learning more vivid and engaging, but the best scenarios are the learner's actual problems or challenges.

Here are some examples:

Topic of the Learning Experience	Design
How to write better performance reviews	If they can, have learners bring to class a performance review that they need to write, and structure the activities and discussions around writing that review. At the end of the class, each learner will have a draft of a real performance review.
Filling out tax returns	Have students start their own returns.
Speaking Thai	Have learners think about things they'd like to be able to talk about (their kids, music, food, politics, introducing themselves), and have them work on ways to talk about those topics in Thai.
Project management	Have learners bring their own project documents and project concerns, and be ready to discuss those concerns, and have them work on solutions to those problems as part of the class.

This set of tactics does a few useful things. First, it gets the learners imagining how they can use the material in their own world. They start picturing the possibilities and figuring out how to deal with obstacles.

Second, it lets the learner get some practice with their own material when there is still support to help iron out snags.

Third, the learners have now made an investment. Behavioral economists talk about sunk cost and loss aversion. People have a strong reluctance to discard something that they've already invested in.

Fourth, they are ready to go when they get back to the real world. There's always a barrier to starting something new, and if the learner has already scaled part of that barrier, then there's less effort required from them as they continue. So, whenever it's feasible, have the learners apply the subject matter to their own situations.

SOCIAL PROOF

We've already talked about how a good way to attract the elephant's attention is to tell it that all the other elephants are doing it.

But social proof (as discussed in Chapter 5—you remember, the tendency of people to base their own actions on the actions of others around them) is useful not only for attracting attention. It's also really good for encouraging the behavior.

Additionally, we can't be experts on everything, so a good tool—often an effective shortcut—is to turn to or to cite people whose opinions we respect, and whose advice we seek. If those people tell us that something is useful, we are much more likely to try it ourselves. I have folks who, if they tell me to go check something out, I'll do it without much question, because I trust their opinion:

I've worked on a number of client projects where, at the beginning of the course, there has been a "this is a really important initiative" message from the CEO, or the relevant vice president, which is fine. It's good to know a project is known and supported at the top—gives it a feeling of authority, I guess you'd say.

But really, who is, or should be, the actual authority figure when it comes to doing your actual job? Is it the CEO, or is the person in the next cubicle who has five times as much experience as you? If you are shopping on Amazon, whose opinion are you going to really value—the publisher, whose blurb assures you this author is a GENIUS, or the 19 readers who've said "meh…"?

In the Project ALERT drug-prevention project, they use influential opinion leaders to talk to kids about reasons not to do drugs. Now, granted, the term "influential opinion leaders" means different things in different situations, but if you are a 13-year old schoolkid, whose opinion would you most value?

Parents?   Teachers?   Police officers?   16-year-olds?

Obviously, that depends on the 13-year old, but as a general rule, for middle-schoolers, high-school kids are pretty much the arbiters of what is and is not cool. To that end, Project ALERT doesn't spend a lot of time with lectures from adult authority figures, but makes good use of teenagers talking about their experiences, and how to make good choices.

So think about it—given your subject matter, who are the really influential people in your organization or in the eyes of your target audience? How can you make those opinions visible? Here are a few possibilities:

- **Have people describe successes with the process, procedure, or skill.** These descriptions can be presented on an intranet, a discussion forum, in email blasts, or through any delivery methods already available in an organization. If possible, you could create mini feature stories about the person who is using the process to good effect—that person could be the star of the show.

- **Engage opinion leaders first.** Involve your opinion leaders in the planning of the endeavor and in the creation and design of the learning experience. Can you have them lend case studies, or agree to champion the undertaking? Can you have them mentor others?
- **Make progress visible.** Many games put up leader boards to show who is really killing it. While shaming low-performing people publicly is counterproductive, having a way to acknowledge those who are succeeding can help encourage others.

VISCERAL MATTERS

The elephant is not influenced only by outside forces like peer encouragement. The elephant is also swayed by direct experience and strong emotion. Direct visual choices and visceral experiences can sway the choices that learners make.

For example, in the cake-or-fruit-salad choice from Chapter 5, people were more likely to pick the cake if they actually had it in front of them. If the choice was more abstract, they had more self-control about choosing fruit salad.

or

If we thought back to our texting-while-driving issue, how could we make the experience more visceral or direct for people?

Here are a couple of ways this has been done:

- *The New York Times* created an interactive game to test how good you are at changing lanes while distracted by a text message. It measures how much your reaction time slows down when you are trying to deal with distractions. You get direct experience with your own limitations. Unfortunately, it's not a very realistic simulation (you change lanes by pressing numbers on the keyboard).
- In 2009, the Gwent Police Force in Wales sponsored the creation of a video showing teenage girls in a car. The driver is texting, and while she does, the car drifts across the median line and strikes an oncoming car. A horrific accident ensues, and you see every graphic detail.

These are both visceral procedures—one involving direct experience and one an emotionally wrenching video. There's no data I can find on the outcomes of either solution, unfortunately. However, I can tell you from personal experience: I do flash on the memory of the video if I'm ever tempted to break my own rule against texting while driving.

While scare tactics often fail to change behavior, there does seem to be some benefit to strong visceral experiences, although more research is needed in this area.

YOU NEED TO FOLLOW UP

All of the above suggestions and strategies can be useful, but possibly the most important idea to keep in mind is this:

Change is a process, not an event.

Any time you want learners to change their behavior, it's a process, and *it needs to be reinforced.*

The ways to reinforce the change are all the things we've already discussed, so this isn't a new idea at this point, but it's still an important point. Be patient! Even if all your learners start out with the best intentions, making a conscious effort to implement the new solution or innovation, they are likely to trickle off if the change isn't reinforced. Always consider how that change will be reinforced over the long term.

 ## SUMMARY

- There are two kinds of motivation that learning designers need to consider: motivation to learn, and motivation to do.
- When you hear "I know, but...," that's a clue that you'll probably need to design for motivation.
- "I know, but..." frequently comes up when there is a delayed reward or consequence.
- We learn from experience, but it can be a problem if we learn the *wrong thing* from experience.
- Change is hard.
- We are creatures of habit—irritating for the short-term learning curve, but potentially useful if we can help learners develop a new habit.
- You may be able to influence your learners, but you can't control them.
- Learning designs should show the learners how something new is useful and easy to use.
- Try to ensure your learners get the opportunity to observe and personally try new processes or procedures.
- Learners need to feel a sense of self-efficacy with the new challenge or skill.
- Use opinion leaders as examples.
- Visceral experiences may have more impact than abstract ones, although the research on this topic is ongoing.

REFERENCES

Bandura, Albert. 1977. Self-efficacy: Toward a unifying theory of behavioral change. *Psychological Review* 84: 191-215.

Dance, Gabriel, Tom Jackson, and Aron Pilhofer. 2009. Gauging Your Distraction. *New York Times.* www.nytimes.com/interactive/2009/07/19/technology/20090719-driving-game.html

Davis, F. D. 1989. Perceived usefulness, perceived ease of use, and user acceptance of information technology. *MIS Quarterly* 13(3): 319–340.

Dweck, Carol S. 2007. The Perils and Promises of Praise. *Educational Leadership* 65 (2): 34–39.

Fogg, BJ. 2011, 2010. Behavior Model (www.behaviormodel.org) and Behavior Grid (www.behaviorgrid.org).

Mueller, Claudia M. and Carol S. Dweck. 1998. Intelligence praise can undermine motivation and performance. *Journal of Personality and Social Psychology* 75: 33-52.

PSA Texting and Driving, U.K. 2009. www.youtube.com/watch?v=8I54mlKOkVw. Described at www.gwent.police.uk/leadnews.php?a=2172.

Rogers, Everett M. 1962. *Diffusion of Innovations.* Glencoe: Free Press. Most recently revised 2003 (5th edition).

DESIGN FOR ENVIRONMENT

(In which we learn that some stoves are smarter than others, and that proximity matters)

ENVIRONMENT GAPS

One of my very first professional jobs was doing training for the customer service call center in a financial services company (and yes, this job was just as rockin' as it sounds, but it was also a really good learning experience).

The job of being a customer service rep (CSR) in this call center was pretty demanding. Not only did you deal with grumpy people all day, but you also had to coax customer information from several different computer systems.

The reps had to constantly flip back and forth between the accounting systems and the credit systems and the customer records systems for four different divisions, and most of these systems didn't talk to each other. Their computer screens looked like this:

As you can imagine, it took a while to get really good at this. We figured that, despite our best training efforts, it took about six months before a rep was really comfortable navigating all the systems, and answering most customer questions.

It was also an entry-level position, and due to a lot of expansion, reps could often transfer out to other, better paid, positions in the company pretty rapidly.

So it worked kind of like this:

> *Amount of time to get a CSR up to speed = About 6 months*
>
> *Amount of time to before a CSR transferred out of the department = About 6 months*

You can see the difficulty here.

While there were undoubtedly many things we could do to improve the training experience, that wasn't really the problem. There were too many weird exceptions, and too many instances where reps had to learn and remember bizarre strings of procedures to get the right information to answer the customer's question.

Actually, it was kind of amazing that the reps were able to get good at their jobs at all, given the difficulty of the environment. That they did was a testament to practice and determination.

The real gaps weren't knowledge, or skills, or motivation. The real gaps were in the environment. That's what we needed to fix.

KNOWLEDGE IN THE WORLD

Donald Norman, in his fantastic, classic design book *The Design of Everyday Things*, has a chapter called *Knowledge in the Head and in the World*. In it, he talks about taking the burden off of memory (knowledge in the head) and putting that information into the environment (knowledge in the world).

The example he gave is his stovetop, which was set up somewhat similar to this:

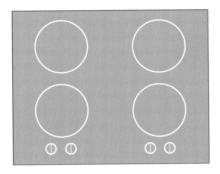

There are four burners and four dials, but can you tell which dial lights which burner? At best, you can narrow it down to one of two options, and then you either a) take the time to figure out which one it is each time you use the stove, b) memorize which is which, or c) guess and hope you don't set anything on fire.

Norman then points out that there are ways to design stoves where you don't have to remember anything. For example, can you tell which dial goes with which burner on this stovetop?

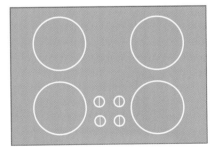

Changing the design of the environment can make knowledge or skills gaps disappear. By taking the knowledge and embedding it in the world, we can vastly reduce the amount of information we ask our learners to pick up and carry around.

LEARNING THE *RIGHT* THINGS

It's not practical or appropriate to take *all* the burden off the learners, but there are things that both people and technology are good at and bad at, and they are mostly not the same things.

Things That (Most) People Are Bad At	Things That (Most) People Are Good At
Differential calculus	Walking in the woods
Loan calculations and amortizations	Understanding what other people are saying
Retaining and retrieving large strings of information	Recognizing and responding to emotions

Things That Technology Is Bad At	Things That Technology Is Good At
Walking in the woods	Differential calculus
Understanding what other people are saying	Loan calculations and amortizations
Recognizing and responding to emotions	Retaining and retrieving large strings of information

Improving the environment is about clearing out as much of the stuff that learners don't really need to carry around in their heads, and instead letting them focus on the things that only they are able to do.

PROXIMITY MATTERS

One of the things you need to consider when putting knowledge into the world is the proximity of the knowledge to the task.

By this I mean, how far from the task does the learner have to go to get the knowledge?

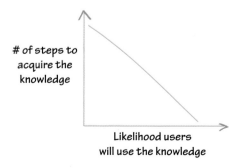

Admittedly, that chart is my estimation (not based on actual data), but if the learner has to find an instruction manual, open it to the table of contents, scan for the subject, turn to the section, consult the index, and finally find the information they are looking for, then they are probably going to skip it and ask the person sitting next to them instead—a valid strategy, unless the person next to them doesn't know, or would prefer to not be interrupted.

The closer you can get the knowledge to the place the user is going to use it, the more likely they'll actually do so. We'll look at a few different kinds of ways to put knowledge into the environment, based on their proximity to the task:

- Resources
- Triggers or prompts
- Embedded behaviors

PUTTING RESOURCES IN THE WORLD

There are many ways to put knowledge resources into the environment. It's beyond the scope of this book to go into huge detail on this, but we'll just take a look at a few examples (for more on this topic, any of Allison Rossett's books on job aids are excellent resources).

JOB AIDS

Job aids are typically prompts, instructions, or memory aids that are readily available to help people accomplish tasks.

Here's one of my favorite job aids:

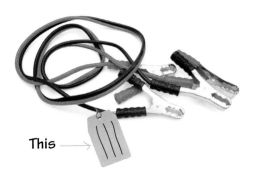

This ⟶ \\\\\

This unimportant-looking yellow tag on my jumper cables gives me a quick reminder how not to electrocute myself while jumping a car battery. I've probably jumped a few dozen batteries over the years, but it's typically been several months to years between instances, and I find it very reassuring to be able to consult the little tag right there.

This is a great example of the importance of proximity. If there wasn't a little tag attached to my jumper cables, I'd probably be tempted to just wing it, rather than trying to get the information elsewhere.

A colleague of mine, Dave Ferguson, talks about how job aids can act as *training wheels,* which he describes as something to "guide the novice so that he produces results similar to those of an expert without having to internalize all the knowledge the expert has." (Ferguson 2009)

Dave goes on to explain that job aids, like an airline's preflight checklist, can also act as *guard rails* to "protect you from incorrect or unsafe performance."

The jumper cables do a little of both for me. I could probably do it right without the tag, but it's nice to have the reminder, and I check my performance against the instructions to avoid the aforementioned electrocution.

In the "nice to have a reminder" category, reference keys can provide simple, useful information that some people might really need and that might just make others feel more "supported," knowing they can double-check themselves at a time when they may not really be thinking clearly. For example, the simple icons on a map legend or a wall placard in an airport may seem obvious when you think clearly about them, but more unusual ones may require explanation.

Here are a few other types of job aids:

- **Decision trees** If a process has very specific and predetermined decision points, then giving people a logical step-by-step way to navigate those decisions can significantly improve learner performance.

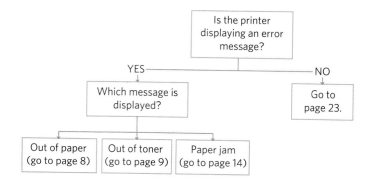

Related to decision are process diagrams and even org charts.

- **Reference information** People aren't good at remembering long sequences of numbers or detailed lists, so providing learners quick, easy access to those types of information can make a big difference in the efficiency of the process.

Loan Program	< 5% Down	5-15% Down	> 15% Down
15-year fixed	#.##%	#.##%	#.##%
20-year fixed	#.##%	#.##%	#.##%
30-year fixed	#.##%	#.##%	#.##%

- **Augmented reality** An interesting type of job aid that's starting to gain traction is *augmented reality*, which puts a virtual information "layer" over the real world, that can be viewed using virtual reality headsets or the camera on mobile devices.

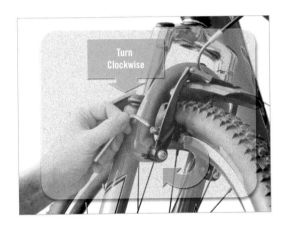

SUPPLY CACHING

Frequently, when your learners are first learning something, they are over-whelmed with detail, so figuring out ways to cache some of that information and provide it later can be really useful.

For example, I've been trying to learn Adobe Illustrator so I can edit the graphics that appear in this book. I'm still pretty much a novice (I know enough to break things), but I love watching experts use the program. A graphic designer friend of mine is a wizard at Illustrator, and when he uses it his fingers dance all over the keyboard. I think he knows dozens of keyboard shortcuts that he learned to speed up his performance.

Trying to learn keyboard shortcuts while I try to master the basics of Illustrator is probably too much for me, but as I go along I will want that information.

A common, easy job aid in the training world is a card that has the keyboard shortcuts on it that I could keep at my desk.

Many software makers have done a nice thing, though, that leaves that infor-mation in an even handier place:

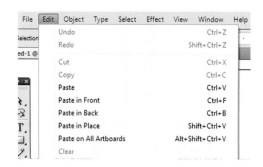

Basically, this information is placed as close to the actual behavior as possible—while I am in the act of using the Edit menu to select the "Paste in Place" command, I have an informational prompt that lets me know there's a shortcut key for that particular command, if I would care to use it in the future.

Another example of this that I've always liked is in the interface of the tax software I used to use. Whatever page of the tax entry program I was on would have some handy questions in the side column like "What is the alternative minimum tax?" I could look it up, but the real strength of that particular interface was that it typically showed only the 5–6 questions that were most relevant at the time. Another nice tactic was to put the message "This is unusual" next to obscure tax questions, so I would know that they were probably not relevant to me. This program has also started crowdsourcing, by capturing and displaying other users' questions and answers. Leveraging your learners' knowledge through wikis or forums can be an invaluable source of information.

PUTTING PROMPTS/TRIGGERS IN THE WORLD

There's an academic/researcher named Peter Gollwitzer who spends a lot of time on the idea of implementation intentions. Basically, he explains implementation intention as follows:

> *Implementation intentions are if-then plans that connect anticipated critical situations with responses that will be effective in accomplishing one's goals. Whereas...goals specify what one wants to do/achieve (i.e., "I intend to perform behavior X!"...), implementation intentions specify the behavior that one will perform in the service of goal achievement if the anticipated critical situation is actually encountered (i.e. "If situation Y occurs, then I will initiate goal-directed behavior Z!").*

Basically, if you are trying to quit smoking, you need more than the goal ("I'm going to stop smoking")—you need the implementation intention of how to actually do it.

So you could say:

> *If I get a craving, I will distract myself.*

You have situation Y ("If I get a craving") and behavior Z ("I will distract myself"). This is more effective than just the goal ("I will quit smoking"). But you can make it much more effective by being specific:

> *If I get twitchy for a cigarette, I will chew gum.*
> *If stress makes me want a cigarette, I will call my sister.*
> *When I want an afternoon smoke break, I will take a 5-minute walk outside.*

So could you use this as a tool in training classes/applications? I'm specifically thinking about a lot of the soft-skill training that goes on—single-event training that has historically not led to much behavioral change. How many times have you learned about a good idea/tool/concept and never done anything with it?

How about an activity where you have people identify their own anticipated critical situations, and have a specific behavioral strategy for responding ("When I have problem X with my difficult employee, I will do Y")? Remember, the specificity is crucial to success.

The way this relates to environment is to then figure out a way to put the triggers in the real world. Are there ways to take the prompts or triggers from implementation intentions and give them a physical presence in your learners' environments?

This is already being done for some things:

This is both a good and bad example. Some research (e.g., Johnson 2003) suggests that hand-washing signs do increase the number of people who wash their hands, but that it clearly doesn't work with everybody. It's also likely that people habituate to these signs pretty quickly (one way to offset habituation is to use novelty—for example, Mr. T could remind you to wash your hands one week, and a Schoolhouse Rock character could prompt you the next).

Still, prompts in the environment can increase behavior, and it's likely that having your learners create their own prompts would be a more effective way to encourage behavior.

Another of my favorite examples of putting a prompt into the environment is this example from the pretzel shops that you often find in shopping malls. They have pretzel-shaped markings on their countertops that look kind of like this:

This handy guide is built right into the countertop. You just roll the dough out to the length and thickness of one of the lines (for larger and smaller pretzels) and then wrap it on top of the appropriate pretzel shape.

This is an example of a prompt that not only triggers the behavior, but also provides guidance on how to perform the task. Experienced pretzel-makers probably ignore the markings, but the guides are an excellent example of how to embed "training wheels" into the environment for new employees.

PUTTING BEHAVIORS IN THE WORLD

Have you ever seen the person in the small food stand or diner who just *knows* how long things take? Maybe she can start a drink pouring at the soda machine, turn to ring a customer, and know exactly how long she has before she needs to turn around and keep the cup from overfilling. That's the sign of an expert who really knows their job, and has internalized that knowledge over time.

More common these days is the evidence of that knowledge being embedded into the world.

The type of soda machine shown below is pretty common. The employee can put in the cup and just press a single button for small, medium, or large.

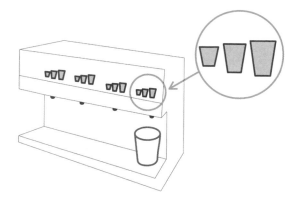

This machine allows even a brand-new employee to perform this particular task at the same level as a seasoned veteran, without having to go through a slow learning process. The information and, even more important, the behavior has been embedded in the machine, rather than in the learner.

In the call center example I described at the beginning of the chapter, one of the tasks the customer service reps had to do was evaluate people for loan programs. This involved getting information from the customer about their homes, the total value, the loan amount, and the amount of down payment. They then had to calculate the percentage of the down payment and use the other information to whittle down which loan program was the right one. They then had to flip over to a different system to calculate the monthly payment for the customer. This wasn't a hugely difficult task, but it did have 9 or 10 steps, and making an error on any of those steps could lead to the wrong program and payment amount, and it did take learners a while to master the process.

To solve the problem, we eventually added an interface layer to the system that required the reps to ask only three questions of the customer and enter two numerical values, and the loan program and monthly payment amount would be calculated for them. The question and fields were on the screen, so the reps could just read them to the customer—they no longer needed to memorize the questions or the steps of the process. Accuracy rates went up significantly when this system was in place, and a lot of the knowledge that reps had previously needed to learn was now embedded in the system.

One of the things that this system successfully accomplished was to shift the burden from a recall problem to a recognition one.

Do you remember how, in Chapter 4, we looked at recall being a better way to test knowledge than recognition? That was true in learning or assessment situations, but when you are designing for environment, the exact opposite is true, and for the same reason—because recognition is easier.

Electronic or Not?

A lot of examples given in this chapter are electronic, and certainly there are a lot of advantages to electronic job aids and references (ease of updating, searchability).

Technology is doing amazing things with giving people access to information anywhere, but sometimes a simple solution can be the best one. One of my personal favorite simple solutions is the Freedom Trail in Boston.

If you want to get all the tourists to all the historic sites in Boston safely and efficiently, you could arrange tours, or provide maps, or you could create a slick GPS-based guide application that people could access on their smart phones.

Or you could just put a big red line down the street.

In Boston there is a red line that tourists can follow through the entire historic district, which will take them to the most significant historical tourist sites. This trail goes for miles, and all people have to do is start at one end and follow the line. It's hard for anyone to misunderstand, it doesn't require operating-system compatibility or cell phone reception, and it's a beautiful example of putting knowledge in the world.

CLEARING THE PATH

Our environment is a massive influence on our behavior. For example, consider the issue of rising obesity rates. We all know that rates of obesity are steadily increasing and that this problem poses health risks to a significant segment of the population.

So, if rates of obesity are substantially higher than they were 30–50 years ago, what's changed in that time? We tend to see obesity as a personal issue—caused by an individual's choices and behaviors—but that doesn't really explain the larger numbers. People aren't significantly different than they were 50 years ago, evolutionarily speaking. We have the same brains, and the same basic natures; those haven't changed. What has changed radically is the environment we live in. 50 years ago, soda came in 8-ounce servings, dinner plates weren't 12 inches across, a family of four had only one car between them, and nobody worried about how many hours of screen time they got in a day.

The point is, environment is a very powerful regulator of behavior, and if people aren't doing the right thing, it's important to look at ways to improve the environment.

Always ask these questions:

- Can we make the process simpler?
- Can we make the system better?
- What barriers are keeping people from succeeding?

You want to walk through the process step by step looking for problems. You particularly want to keep an eye peeled for frustration points, because the more you can do to smooth out the journey, the more likely your learners are to succeed.

Ask "why are we doing it that way?" at each step. If you hear the words "that's the process" or "that's how we've always done it," then that should be a big screaming alarm telling you to scrutinize that step and make sure it's really necessary instead of just being a habit or a tradition.

THE BIG QUESTION

Here's the really crucial question to ask yourself when designing for environment:

> *What's everything else we could do (besides training) that will allow learners to succeed?*

For this, I recommend a full-on, whiteboard-scribbling, multi-colored sticky note, no idea is a bad idea, free-for-all brainstorm session. Then consider all those solutions. If laminating wall-size posters, or making cookies, or flying in experts, or getting an on-site masseuse, or setting up a wiki, or buying everyone Magic-8 Balls (as decision-making aids, of course) will help the process, then consider the cost-benefit of those notions.

To get more detail, you should also ask "what could we do beforehand to make people more ready?" and "what could we do afterwards to reinforce?"

SUMMARY

- Instead of trying to put all the knowledge into the learners' heads, try to figure out if some of the knowledge can be put into the environment instead.
- Activities that are particularly difficult for humans to master are good candidates for embedding into the environment.
- Proximity matters—try to get the knowledge as close to the behavior as possible.
- When designing for environment, remember that recognizing the right option is easier than recalling it.
- Don't just teach learners how to do a process; look at the process to see if there's any way to streamline it to make it simpler and easier to perform.

REFERENCES

Ferguson, David. 2009. Job aids: training wheels and guard rails. *Dave's Whiteboard March 31, 2009*. http://www.daveswhiteboard.com/archives/1939.

Gollwitzer, P. M. 2006. Successful goal pursuit. In *Psychological science around the world* 1: 143–159, Q. Jing, H. Zhang, and K. Zhang, Eds. Philadelphia: Psychology Press.

Gollwitzer, P. M., K. Fujita, and G. Oettingen. 2004. Planning and the implementation of goals. In *Handbook of self-regulation: Research, theory, and applications*, R. F. Baumeister and K. D. Vohs, Eds. New York: Guilford Press.

Jeffery, Robert W. and Jennifer Utter. 2003. The Changing Environment and Population Obesity in the United States. *Obesity Research* 11, DOI: 10.1038/oby.2003.221.

Johnson, H. D., D. Sholoscky, K. L. Gabello, R. V. Ragni, and N. M. Ogonosky. 2003. Gender differences in handwashing behavior associated with visual behavior prompts. *Perceptual and Motor Skills* 97: 805–810.

Norman, Donald. 1990. *The Design of Everyday Things.* New York: Doubleday Business. Originally published as *The Psychology of Everyday Things.* 1988. New York: Basic Books.

CONCLUSION

(In which we say,
"Thanks for sticking it out, folks!")

Small children are natural learners—they just suck information out of their environment through curiosity and play.

Somewhere along the way, we lose that. We learn that learning is serious business, and that it's hard and effortful.

Learning designers have an opportunity to defy that notion, and create marvelous, interesting, relevant learning environments. We can't *make* anybody learn, but we can make much better learning environments for them.

Lately, I've been listening to a series of podcasts on storytelling (www.storywonk.com), and one of the points they continually make is that even incidental characters are the heroes of their own stories.

I've been thinking about that in connection to learning design. We typically design for audiences of "learners," but each individual learner is the hero of their own learning journey. We just need to ensure they have everything they need to move along the path.

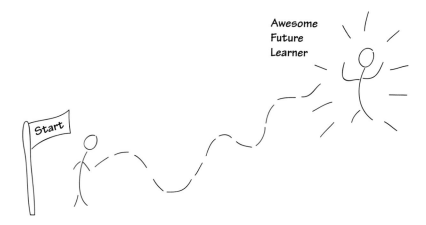

It seems fitting to end the book with a quote from the fantastic Kathy Sierra, who has been hugely influential on me as a learning designer:

> *"Kicking ass is more fun regardless of the task. It's more fun to know more. It's more fun to be able to do more. It's more fun to be able to help others do more."*

INDEX